Praise for *LEADERSHIP STORM*

"*Leadership Storm* is an essential guide for anyone who wants to lead with vision and impact."

—**SAM REESE,** chief executive officer, Vistage Worldwide, Inc.

LEADERSHIP STORM

LEADERSHIP STORM

A TRAINING MANUAL

MARY SEARCY BIXBY

GREENLEAF
BOOK GROUP PRESS

Published by Greenleaf Book Group Press
Austin, Texas
www.gbgpress.com

Distributed by Greenleaf Book Group

For ordering information or special discounts for bulk purchases, please contact Greenleaf Book Group at PO Box 91869, Austin, TX 78709, 512.891.6100.

Design and composition by Greenleaf Book Group
Cover design by Greenleaf Book Group

Publisher's Cataloging-in-Publication data is available.

Hardcover ISBN: 979-8-88645-394-2

Paperback ISBN: 979-8-88645-468-0

eBook ISBN: 979-8-88645-395-9

To offset the number of trees consumed in the printing of our books, Greenleaf donates a portion of the proceeds from each printing to the Arbor Day Foundation. Greenleaf Book Group has replaced over 50,000 trees since 2007.

Printed in the United States of America on acid-free paper

25 25 27 28 29 30 31 32 10 9 8 7 6 5 4 3 2 1

First Edition

To the many Leaders who strive to preserve professional values that ensure organizational quality and performance excellence for the future.

CONTENTS

FOREWORD

ADDRESSING CLIMATE CHANGE, securing our nation's energy independence, preserving access to clean water, improving air quality, and being a careful steward of our most important resources are my passions. Without taking responsible action today, we risk the well-being of future generations. As a husband, father of three, and grandfather of five and counting, I am reminded every day of my need to get it right when it comes to the work I do.

Effective leadership is at the center of creating lasting change within organizations that have the potential to better the lives of countless people. As the former chairman of the board for Altus Schools Charter School of San Diego (CSSD), I've seen how leadership done right has the power to positively disrupt entire industries entrenched in unskillful practices and attitudes.

I joined the board in 2012 because of my desire to use my expertise to improve public education, which is ground zero for change. In order to address the country's and world's biggest challenges, we need to prepare today's young people who will be charged to solve tomorrow's problems. Thus teaching our nation's children to think critically, understand the environment around them, and value lifelong learning are mission-critical tasks to bring about the secure, sustainable future that has been the focus of my professional pursuits.

I have worked closely with Mary Searcy Bixby and have admired her unflagging commitment to leadership, which includes heading her organizations, being at the forefront of her industry, and mentoring future generations of leaders.

Under her extraordinary stewardship, Altus Schools Charter School of San Diego was awarded the prestigious Malcolm Baldrige National Quality Award in 2015 and again in 2021, establishing CSSD as a national role model for education. CSSD was the first and only K through 12 school to earn the recognition twice in the award's thirty-three-year history.

Having served in the US Navy with distinction for over thirty-two years and receiving the Navy Distinguished Service Medal and the Presidential Award for Leadership in Federal Energy Management from President George W. Bush in 2005, I retired from the navy and was appointed vice president for Business Services and Administration at the University of San Diego. I then became the president and executive director of the Center for Sustainable Energy. After more than five years of leading California's most respected energy center, I took the helm of the nonprofit I Love A Clean San Diego, where I led thousands toward a better, cleaner environment.

From the armed forces to civilian life, I've led large organizations and countless men and women and worked closely with leaders across multiple industries. I have proudly served and continue to serve on a number of local and national-level boards, and I must admit that Mary Searcy Bixby's remarkable ability to realize her ambitious vision of breaking the public education status quo and bringing about innovation in one of the most entrenched industries in our country is a testament to the power of American entrepreneurship.

For CSSD to succeed against an often-adversarial backdrop critical of charter schools has required leadership that is strong, politically astute, ethical, disciplined, driven, and compassionate. To face the fierce headwinds that any organization seeking to bring about cutting-edge change faces requires unrelenting courage and high emotional intelligence. Mary consistently demonstrates these qualities.

For Mary to elevate CSSD to the pinnacle of exceptional success has required teamwork. By creating a deep bench of high-performing board members and leaders within her organization, Mary and her team have been able to achieve educational outcomes that would have been otherwise impossible to accomplish.

Leadership Storm is a training manual for those as passionate as I am about leadership and its ability to improve teams, organizations and the constituents they serve, industries, and society at large. As a leader who has worked closely with this book's author, I can attest to the transformative power within the pages of this book.

Whether you're a leader, an aspiring one, or seeking to instill leadership excellence throughout an organization, by following the lessons in *Leadership Storm,* you'll learn how to unleash the limitless potential that is the hallmark of all great leaders. If you're ready to leave an enduring legacy, then your journey to excellence starts here.

—RADM Len Hering Sr., USN, Retired

INTRODUCTION

A NEAR-ENDLESS NUMBER of books cover the topic of leadership, drawing in readers who are fascinated and interested in the subject. During previous decades, most CEOs and entrepreneurs were behind the scenes, overseeing massive projects. Nowadays, the public follows their high-profile lives similar to famous politicians and Hollywood celebrities.

The widespread coronavirus lockdowns starting in 2020 broke the professional status quo. The daily Monday-through-Friday commute had been an American tradition for decades. Suddenly, with state and local shelter-in-place mandates, the workplace shifted from business parks and tall buildings to the home office.

Professionals had to quickly adapt, and they relied on their employers for guidance. Meanwhile, leaders bore the weight of heading organizations and accomplishing objectives during unprecedented times. Years later, businesses continue to address the ripple effects of a global crisis organizations had never faced before.

Companies that want their employees back in the office are struggling with a workforce now preferring to work from home. The possibility of further lockdowns in the future has put both businesses and their staff on edge. Swaths of the global workforce have descended into depression. And the learning loss the next generation of employees experienced during their school years will require leaders to prepare future staff beyond what was needed before.

Given the widespread allure of leadership and the challenges leaders face against the headwinds of global events and technological advances, I thought deeply about how this book would contribute to the advancement of the subject.

In writing my previous book, *Charter Storm*, my coauthor of that book, Dr. Tom Davis, and I met with leaders from all over the country. We interviewed men and women with track records of high accomplishment that span decades. Their innovations have improved the lives of countless people.

Through our investigation and my own leadership journey, I was driven to equip leaders, both present and emerging, to achieve greatness. With technology and geopolitical events rapidly changing the societies in which we live and work, effective leadership requires a skill set more demanding now than at any time before.

Imagine a five-year-old today being a leader in twenty years. The world he or she will live in will be dramatically different from the one we inhabit presently. Addressing today's and tomorrow's challenges for my organization has been my professional life work, as has been equipping emerging leaders to achieve excellence.

Within the organization I founded, we've nurtured leaders that remain loyal. Their steadfastness has allowed us to take advantage of the training we've given these leaders. This has been a point of pride and fueled our high accomplishments. Instead of a lucky outcome or mere coincidence, our results have come as a result of a specific culture in the leadership guidance we've embedded throughout our organization.

For us, leadership is not restricted to C-level posts. Because the CEO, CFO, COO, CBO, and more have authority and ultimate responsibility for the outcomes of their departments, their leadership role is clear. But beyond them, leaders may exist at any level within an organization. According to our vision, leadership is a reciprocal relationship between leaders and followers.

High-performing organizations have both positional and non-positional leaders who practice leadership every day and at every level. The clearest examples of positional leadership are in the C-suite. Non-positional leaders may not have the organizational title but nonetheless demonstrate leadership. Both have been the foundation of our organization's success.

Throughout this book, I also distinguish between leaders and managers. All leaders benefit from having management skills. But Leaders (with a capital *L*) go beyond this. They innovate and break the status quo if necessary to create lasting positive change.

By modeling our vision of Leadership throughout our organization, we have created a strong and enduring workforce. This means, no matter what personnel changes take place, our operations run seamlessly and without disruption.

Our Leadership strategy has equipped our organization to thrive within a highly regulated industry that changes at breakneck speed. Within these pages, you'll learn the practices that have benefited us and are essential to run any exceptional organization. In addition, you'll read about remarkable Leaders who, in an outstanding way, practice the Leadership elements described in these pages.

With challenges both known and unknown, successfully leading will be harder than ever in the years and decades to come. Whether you're currently in a leadership position, aspire to occupy one, or seek to mentor others, this book will serve as your guide.

Leadership Storm is a training manual providing clear, practical wisdom that prepares you, those you mentor, and your organization to lead through times of dizzying change. My hope is to inform you on your Leadership journey. I seek to provide ideas that will help you become a Leader. And if you're one already, I provide you with tools along your path of continual and relentless improvement.

Chapter 1

NO ONE BECOMES CEO BY ACCIDENT

It is better to fail in originality, than to succeed in imitation.

—**HERMAN MELVILLE**, "Hawthorne and His Mosses"

TODAY'S LEADERS ALL began as children, each one born with talents, skills, and potential. A successful CEO often shares the story of her beginnings. Her bedroom was her tiny paradise. Her windows were covered with blinds and sheer curtains that allowed rays of light to come through that created cloudlike patterns on the floor. Pink bedspread, carpet, and walls made a delicate atmosphere that provided the perfect background for her to dream about her future.

Like a movie unfolding before her eyes, this CEO-to-be, an only child, played quietly and alone. With the toy typewriter she received for Christmas, she envisioned what grown-up life would look like for her. From her earliest memories, daydreams were full of executive-level trappings:

ascending a staircase to an airplane ready to take her to her next important destination, a microphone prepared to amplify her address to a large audience, and a suitcase in her hand packed with her belongings for the meeting she was headed to.

She was a little person with big dreams. Once, she imagined herself typing while sitting at the head of a long conference room table, surrounded by deeply engaged people. Their eyes were fixed on her, waiting for what she would say next. Her dream stopped there.

In her reverie, she felt the independence, boldness, and power of her position. She and her work were both grand and important. From a young age, she knew what she wanted. While she couldn't describe it back then, upon present reflection, she realizes she had imagined herself a leader.

■ ■ ■

Before taking a deep dive into what being a Leader is, let's begin by exploring what it isn't. With so much information about leadership available in any internet search, we wind up with as many definitions of leadership as self-proclaimed leaders themselves.

Too often, leadership is equated with the dark side of strength, which is rooted in domination, intimidation, and demanding unquestioned obedience from followers. From maniacal dictators to ruthless CEOs, these leaders command respect through threats and force rather than earning it from acts of selfless courage to benefit others.

Leadership is not merely a series of platitudes. While compelling and thought provoking, they are not the same as actions that generate remarkable results. A magnetic personality and adept public speaking are hallmarks of exceptional leaders. But Leadership moves far beyond words spoken.

You only need to look at countless power-hungry politicians to see how often they make headline-making statements but never follow up or fulfill the promises they make. While some leaders may have begun with an intention to do good, their insatiable hunger for positional power eventually takes priority over any altruistic tendency. With so many examples of individuals representing the dark side of leadership, it's clear why the term is defined in so many ways.

The pursuit of finding our place in the grand scheme of the universe is a frequent human endeavor. Most of us have probably asked ourselves at some point in our lives: Who am I? What can I accomplish? Where do I want to wind up?

While these questions may be common, the depth and energy we put toward answering them vary dramatically. For example, many people may have the aspiration to become a number one, such as the winner of a competition. But what differentiates the person who imagines ascending to high levels of success versus someone who actually succeeds?

Similarly, many people dream of being a leader. This goal may have started when they were young—a child who wanted to be the best in playground games, land the lead in a performance, declare victory in sports, or be the top in his or her class. Or leaders may have had no notion of their future role back when they were children. Yet as adults they crave, desire, and are destined to seek this kind of lifestyle.

I refer to positional leadership as a lifestyle because of the immense amount of responsibility and authority required to run an organization—one that can be summed up with "the buck stops here."

Leaders are held accountable for their actions and outcomes—in good times and bad. And in the event of poor outcomes, leaders receive the blame, even when what happened wasn't their fault.

Meanwhile, not all men and women who reach this level of professional success see their leadership roles as a lifestyle. Perhaps these individuals never intended to become leaders but, by accident or circumstance, found themselves in this position. As a result, they may not feel comfortable with the authority and responsibility they've been charged with. The bottom line is leadership manifests itself in different ways to different people.

So, if leadership can have so many meanings, how do I define it?

First, it is often positional. Today, the term *C-level* is synonymous with leader. The capital C comes from "chief," and the most well-known version of this is the chief executive officer, or CEO. The CEO is vested with the authority and responsibility of any kind of organization.

Many CEOs have advanced degrees and specialty training that reflect their vision and expertise. Examples include engineering, law, medicine, chemistry, and education. They often play a key role in hiring and terminating lower management.

From Amazon's Jeff Bezos to GM's Mary Barra, the heads of today's largest companies have reached celebrity status. Beyond the CEO, C-level also includes many other corporate positions. While CEO has become a term that has spread across many languages, many other C-level titles have emerged, and the list continues to grow over time. The following are examples:

POSITION TITLE	DESCRIPTION
Chief Executive Officer (CEO)	The highest C-level position in a corporation; reports to the board of directors; responsible for the success of the company; often identified with "the buck stops here" and as #1
Chief Business Officer (CBO)	Responsible for all business activities of a corporation, including strategic planning, budget, finance, banking and investments, facilities, etc.
Chief Financial Officer (CFO)	Manages all financial actions of the corporation, such as strategic planning, risk management, records, and financial strengths and weaknesses
Chief Operations Officer (COO)	Responsible for day-to-day administration, including short- and long-term planning and projections; maintains company goals and cultural business perspectives

Next, leadership includes the following four elements:

- A relationship with followers
- A relationship based on influence
- Motivation of followers to bring about real changes
- Development of a mutual purpose

Anyone can be a leader or, at another time or under different circumstances, a follower. Next, followers, as well as leaders, persuade leaders and other followers. Last, leaders and followers change places. This definition takes leadership outside the hierarchy of C-level designations. In other words, positional leadership isn't the only way to be a leader.

For example, imagine that Steve was working on a factory assembly line. He purposefully took the initiative in creating an innovative approach to increase factory efficiency. By actively engaging others in understanding and accepting the change, Steve then endeavored to persuade leaders and followers in implementing a radically better strategy that departed from the status quo. He created a paradigm shift and new approach to doing work. This enterprising team member has displayed the expertise that a leader would, even though he doesn't have a positional leadership title.

The art of effectively using power has always been a challenge for leaders. To do so, they must have confidence, knowledge, and experience. Leaders will use these three characteristics to take their dream or vision, organize it into a sequenced plan, and most importantly, step forward and implement it. Throughout the process, they will measure success and course correct. In order to earn the right to lead, individuals must learn to identify purpose, develop a plan, mobilize their resources, and fulfill their commitments.

The positional designations and the four elements provide a fundamental definition, but Leadership is much more. Neither of these explanations clearly distinguishes between being a manager versus being a leader. In fact, organizations may have leaders in title, but in practice, these men and women are more managers than leaders. These are leader-managers with a lowercase *l*, and they may be at any level. Meanwhile, throughout this book true Leaders are identified with an uppercase *L*. So what's the difference between the two?

An important factor that differentiates Leaders from their leader-managers is the status quo. Leader-managers maintain it. They work with what is, rather than creating effective, deep, and sometimes radical change.

Some of those who find themselves in positional leadership roles may never move past being a leader-manager and may not aspire to anything beyond where they are currently. That's not to say leader-managers lack motivation and neglect to challenge, motivate, or push their team (such as colleagues and employees). Broadly speaking, however, leader-managers often have an "if it ain't broke, don't fix it" attitude, which is the opposite of being change oriented.

As far as leadership style is concerned, leader-managers may follow the same general framework of their colleagues or predecessors. This strategy may have worked for some companies. In fact, organizations may value their traditions and corporate culture to the extent that they seek leader-managers that pledge to uphold the status quo without an uncompromising emphasis on innovation. While this can lead to short-term success, it is not a viable long-term formula. Neglecting to be at the forefront of change will leave an organization unprepared and spell its demise when a new period emerges that disrupts the treasured status quo.

The first Industrial Revolution that took place over 250 years ago is one of humanity's greatest examples of breaking the status quo. It began in England in 1760. This wave of innovation shifted manufacturing from largely labor-intensive products made in homes, workshops, and small factories to large-scale machine production.

From England, the Industrial Revolution swept across Europe and throughout the world. This period resulted in rapid scientific developments and eventually led to the Information Age, which began around 1970 and was marked by an explosion of technology based on data.

Currently, the partnership between humans and machines is heading us toward the current technological wave: artificial intelligence. Yet again, the status quo will be broken, and those who maintain it will be left behind. Ideas that were once breakthrough will become antiquated and useless. And in particular, leaders who aren't agile, don't adjust quickly to change, and fail to lead the charge will see their organizations flounder and most likely fizzle out.

For example, retail giants such as Sears and Kmart dominated the consumer landscape and swallowed up the competition during the Industrial Age. With their national footprints, economies of scale that stretched beyond US borders, and aggressive and successful growth strategies, they became case studies in US corporate prowess.

While they initially stayed competitive at the onset of the Information Age, they are well-known examples of what is called the retail apocalypse, which includes a dizzying long list of both household names and small businesses across the country—many of which represented companies that were once at the cutting edge but wound up closing their doors for good.

Consumer habits have changed, and advertising and marketing are evolving faster than ever. Leaders have understood the danger of the status quo, so they have aggressively course corrected. Meanwhile, leader-managers that hadn't been at the forefront watched revenues shrink and their businesses collapse.

Positionally oriented leaders have the responsibility to prepare their organization to make the changes necessary to thrive as society shifts from one period of development to another while fulfilling their ambition to move up the professional ladder. Succeeding at both is an enormous challenge.

As the retail apocalypse demonstrates, for businesses to successfully transition from the industrial paradigm to the post-industrial model is rare. Automobile manufacturers are an example of an industry shifting from one period to the next. Cars were firmly part of the Industrial Age, and with the advent of the Information Age, they have quickly evolved, being equipped with emerging technology such as GPS, autonomy, hydrogen fuel cells, and electricity. But overall, success stories are rare, and the odds of failure are high.

The automobile industry is highly regulated, and developing a product is costly, as is creating a national distribution network once a car is market ready. These barriers to entry and more have resulted in a long list of promising startups that eventually failed. And even those companies that captured market share over the short term eventually fizzled out.

Today, Cadillac, Ford, BMW, and Toyota are household names. But so were Nash, Studebaker, and Packard in years past. In contrast, Tesla is a remarkable story of overcoming seemingly insurmountable odds and maintaining growth.

Most organizations with roots in the industrial model struggle to move their governance, policy, vision, mission, and practice to meet the demands of the present and future marketplaces. Meanwhile, organizations founded during the Information Age will also need to innovate at unprecedented speed to adapt to AI. They must restructure their organizations to make them agile and responsive in order to make immediate change when necessary.

While leader-managers work within the status quo, Leaders reject it. They strategically strive to make a significant difference for the better. This points to the importance of rejecting the status quo through a rational process.

Unwise change is often worse than no change at all. Rather than reckless and haphazard, the innovation that Leaders achieve comes through their vision based on ethics, creativity, and reason. Like leader-managers, Leaders influence others, especially their leadership teams. But they go beyond this and seek resources that will support their ability to anticipate their customers' future wants and needs.

Leaders endure difficult times and are skilled at triumphing over adversity. They understand that they will face enormous challenges and overcome obstacles at every turn. But while a Leader may do everything possible to prepare for worst cases, a problem may arise beyond even extreme preplanning scenarios. Leaders use their experience, education, intelligence, poise, and confidence to guide them through the high and low (and sometimes very low) points their organizations experience.

Leaders have a need to directly influence and participate in a way that calls them to step up and take control of something that holds clearly defined expectations for their personal sharing of knowledge, expertise, and ultimately power. This process of embracing new and greater responsibility requires them to be tried, tested, and scrutinized. The pressure placed on them is intense, and like hammering heated iron in order to make it stronger and a higher quality, the successful ones are better as a result. Leaders are lifelong learners. They research topics exhaustively and are open-minded to new ideas.

It takes a clear understanding of reality, including the sacrifices, hard work, and determination to realize a Leader's big goals—all of which must align with his or her values, which brings us to the next characteristic of Leaders: They uphold their values *no matter what.*

Unfortunately, some misguided professionals are willing to compromise on their values if it means a faster, easier, or more assured path to goal attainment. They become single-minded success seekers who resort to disingenuous or even unethical deeds, small and big, to meet their objectives.

If a meeting does not interest them or have any self-serving objective, they will excuse themselves in order to take an emergency call or tend to a matter for which they are critically needed. Meanwhile, both events are completely invented. Or when a plan fails, they blame others or outside circumstances and never take responsibility themselves. They are chronic name droppers and claim they have exclusive information reserved for only a select few. Shortsighted in their ambitions, they don't realize or believe that what goes around comes around. What they don't see is that they can commit a string of misdeeds for only so long until they'll face the consequences of their poor judgment.

Throughout your professional journey, you are presented with difficult decisions. One option may provide a short- or long-term gain at the risk of compromising your values. But duplicity, self-serving motives, cutting corners, and laziness will eventually catch up with a leader. At some point, these character flaws will reveal themselves and serve as barriers to goal attainment. In addition, negative actions affect one's demeanor and mood. There are many consequences to being consistently unhappy and self-possessed, including stress and unhealthy professional and personal relationships. Self-serving men and women are not Leaders. They give ambition a bad name.

On the other hand, when value-oriented Leaders display ambition, it is never arrogant. For them, ambition always is associated with being open-minded and curious. It respects the need for incremental steps to create sweeping change or improvement or both. Leaders who display this type of ambition welcome the opportunity to learn from others (such as through mentors and coaches), take risks, be held accountable, and accept reasonable contrarian opinions. They are positive, hopeful, and kind to others, appreciate laughter, and have healthy lifestyles filled with family and friends. When it's time to work, they are detail oriented and invest whatever time is necessary to accomplish a task. This type of ambition drives Leaders in today's most successful organizations and helps them maintain a competitive edge in a fast-paced, results-oriented world.

Leaders not only display ambition, but they also seek it in others. Rather than being threatened by highly motivated team members, they want their leadership teams to have a hunger and desire for excellence. Leaders are confident in their strengths and know their weaknesses. They understand that counting on others' skills is necessary to realize their ambitious goals and create a strong organization.

CEOs welcome quality individuals that push themselves to work effectively through even the most challenging scenarios. They have a vision for themselves and their organizations. In order to realize this, they surround themselves with ambitious value-oriented staff.

Summary

This chapter has centered on positional Leadership as manifested by CEOs and other C-level executives. As we work through future chapters that emphasize critical practices positional leaders such as the CEO use, we must remember that an individual may demonstrate leadership at all levels within an organization. Although not everyone has the authority or responsibility of a C-level executive, everyone can profit by understanding and learning to use strategies related to planning, communication, problem-solving, and other beneficial skills.

Leaders often aspire to high achievement early in their careers. Frequently, their passion and enthusiasm may be viewed by others as unnecessary and unrealistic. Leaders with a vision for what they must achieve generally hold a perspective rooted in their purposeful intention to shape the future.

No matter how challenging or insurmountable obstacles may appear to others, Leaders center their thinking and work on how obvious obstacles may be overcome. They are committed to engaging others in supporting a quest for answers to the toughest questions facing their organization or even society as a whole. A Leader's purpose is to create real, intended change by inspiring activities that make a critical and positive difference. The highest forms of Leadership can result in the positive disruption of the status quo or an entire paradigm shift relating to the change at hand.

In the next chapter, you'll learn timeless practices to maintain high achievement as a Leader during periods of rapid change.

Chapter 2

THE NEW LEADER

There's really no secret to our approach. We keep moving forward—opening up new doors and doing new things—because we're curious. And curiosity keeps leading us down new paths.

—WALT DISNEY

PRIOR TO THE Information Age, the Keystone XL petroleum pipeline extending from Canada to the United States might have been launched in relative obscurity. In fact, in times past, a massive petroleum project could be conceived, approved, developed, and completed before any concerned parties even had time to find out about it—let alone do anything to stop its construction. But when word got out about the Keystone XL Pipeline, groups opposed to it harnessed the power of social media.

From pressuring politicians to organizing massive protests, all major steps to block the pipeline could be performed through a small mobile device. The campaign was so successful that it attracted worldwide media attention. Environmental and Indigenous rights groups criticized the pipeline's impact, and the widespread public outcry sought to stop its construction.

With the public having more access to information than ever, Leaders are held to a higher standard. Those facing strong opposition may have to change course to counter external pressure. Whereas in times past, a company might have been able to get away with decisions rooted in coercion, greed, waste, or a lack of sensitivity to a community's well-being, this is no longer the case.

Compulsion to follow sociopolitical trends may require Leaders to release public statements, disavow groups, and pledge to adhere to popular attitudes. Individuals and groups acting as watchdogs use the tools of today's technology. Many are experts who draw on their skill to guard the public against corporate malfeasance that includes harming the environment and abuses of power.

The Information Age has accelerated societal development at an unprecedented pace. As the world changes, so does its needs, and Leaders must be at the forefront of rapid shifts within the industries they serve. Consider social media as one example. Instagram, TikTok, Facebook, X, and more have created new levels of accountability.

Whether the information is accurate, biased, fraudulent, or irrelevant, it's out there and often must be dealt with. Artificial intelligence has fueled the content and spread of the facts, knowledge, and opinions people consume. The widespread adoption of mobile technology means the voice of the community at large is more powerful than ever. As a result, Leaders must be prepared to be a part of public dialogue. In this chapter, you'll learn to manage your own growth and development. As a result, you'll be better equipped to navigate the stormy seas that surround Leadership today.

In generations past, CEOs were rarely public figures. The heads of large companies may have been famous within their industries, but most were not household names. This provided a degree of privacy that doesn't exist today and could allow organizations to make decisions that would not face the same degree of public scrutiny they do currently.

Leadership today is far less rooted in aspiring toward the positional definition and more about devoting time to being a Leader beyond a C-level job title. Similar to a concert pianist, prima ballerina, astronaut, or professional athlete, leadership is both science and art where becoming a Leader requires immense energy, sacrifice, and stamina.

When Leaders are given two choices—optimism or pessimism—they select the positive path. The opposite is not an option for them. Those with negative dispositions are suspicious of other people and believe they are inherently distrustful. Their perspective is that "it's a dog-eat-dog world," where winning at any cost is the goal. A career ascent done this way is often filled with animosity and fear. And when one finally reaches the mountaintop, it's an unpleasant and isolating place.

A positive worldview is the path of true Leaders. Their trust in others allows them to build effective teams and rely on them, which is how great work is accomplished. While Leaders still are responsible to make tough decisions they would rather avoid or pass along to others, they rely on their positive outlook to guide their course of action. Their optimism results in meaningful relationships. This doesn't mean that conflict will never occur. Humans are complicated and unpredictable. Because Leaders generally trust others, when someone breaks that trust, the feeling of betrayal can run deep. This is particularly the case when it comes to those individuals that Leaders have mentored and guided.

The Plan

While leader-managers can wind up in their posts by circumstance, such as when a position becomes vacant, Leaders never attain their station by accident. They have a goal in mind and a path to arrive there. They understand the importance of struggle and that, without it, there is no progress or accomplishing something grander and larger than themselves. As Bruce Lee said, "Adapt what is useful, reject what is useless, and add what is specifically your own." Those who have become Leaders look back on the struggles and embrace them as part of their journey; without them, they would not have been able to attain their levels of success.

An important aspect of their plan includes intense study. This is critical because it provides guidance to direct one's Leadership aspirations and is an underpinning to one's hopes and dreams. A plan is the guide that indicates the work necessary to becoming a Leader. The more ambitious and laudable the goal, the more necessary to have a plan in place. The following are two steps within the plan.

First, you need to break down the journey you'll take into incremental parts. Success and achievement of any type is built on small, even tiny, steps leading toward a goal. The great change and extraordinary innovation that Leaders advance does not happen by accident.

To bring about the breakthroughs in art, science, politics, and business, as did Leonardo da Vinci, Marie Curie, Abraham Lincoln, and John D. Rockefeller, requires a lifelong commitment to study and experimentation. Famous Leaders are remembered because of the remarkable decisions they made during difficult times, the influence they had on society, and their impact on subsequent generations.

Second, you must acknowledge that it often takes many failures before cracking the code to becoming a Leader. Many have aspired to Leadership but never made it past the incremental steps, sometimes out of fear of failure, indecision, or lack of creativity in confronting challenges. The wise know when to fix an obstacle, when it is best left alone, and when to muster the tremendous strength necessary to move forward. Part of overcoming any obstacle is understanding that circumstances will change, and adaptable Leaders can be ready for those changes. By anticipating change, Leaders can adjust well to it and even celebrate its coming.

Not everyone will agree with your plan, especially if it goes against the status quo, and disputes can result in attacks on you. But the opinions and perceptions others have of you don't define you. While you can spend time determining their value and worth, the bottom line is that others have their reasons for responding to you as they do, and oftentimes, their motivations are impossible to figure out. If your plan rests on solid information, you have considered impartially other input, and you have analyzed the situation, then as a Leader, hold on to the plan, even when others slight you personally.

The Role of Mentorship

An objective perspective is key to gaining clarity about your journey. Begin by looking at the experienced and accomplished. Their paths may not be yours, but they have achieved success in their respective fields.

If you are fortunate enough, you have been connected with a mentor or coach who sees value in you and supports you in your endeavors. These special individuals may have appeared in multiple stages of your life.

In youth sports, you may have had a coach who elevated your performance on and off the field. In high school, you may have had a counselor or youth leader who shed light on your abilities and helped you improve them. A university professor may have provided guidance and introductions that helped you later. Or a supervisor early in your career may have given you the tools that stretched you from being an average employee to an exceptional one.

Mentors and coaches are vital at all levels of your career. If you think they are unnecessary once one reaches the top, consider how many of the nation's CEOs have mentors and coaches. Even at their advanced positions, they still benefit from expressing their thoughts and ideas to an objective third party and receiving a guru's feedback. What is the difference between mentors and coaches?

While coaches are more focused on a person's professional performance and results, mentors are career-development driven, typically work out of the goodness of their hearts, and don't charge fees. Career-development driven means mentors take a more expansive approach; that is, they are helping you assess how you think and see yourself in the world around you. The broader approach can manifest itself in an informal relationship and usually requires a long-term commitment that may span an entire professional career. There is a continual and mutual interaction and exchange of best practices.

Coaches, on the other hand, provide guidance that is more technical, is day-to-day, and relates to the specifics of what you do. They are concerned with your performance and the degree to which you are accomplishing particular tasks. Working closely with their clients, they ask key questions relating to job performance, develop action plans, and establish targets and deadlines. Coaches follow up regularly and help assess the success of a particular plan. Compared to mentors, the coaching relationship is more formal and often is fee based.

The questions mentors and coaches ask are particularly important because it is through wise inquiry that you are pushed to challenge and think beyond your assumptions. This doesn't mean mentors and coaches make decisions for you. Rather, they have a self-actualized perspective that will aid those they assist. They ask the difficult questions and let you determine what, if any, action to take.

Mentors and coaches are intelligent men and women who cannot be schmoozed or flattered into giving false hope to those they guide. While some may be tempted to tell others what they want to hear versus what they should hear, quality mentors and coaches do not take this path.

Giving hard and "tough love" messages isn't easy, but it is necessary to bring about positive and lasting change. Sometimes those they mentor want to be told exactly what to do. While in certain instances this may be the correct course of action, mentors and coaches know that their primary role is to prompt people to find new or different solutions to the problems they encounter—and to ultimately rely on their inner resources for answers. Providing a new and wise perspective from which to tackle a difficult situation is one of the greatest resources a mentor or coach can provide.

Mentors and coaches realize reflecting on their prior experiences gives them a glimpse into the future. By using the past as a guide to tomorrow, they give invaluable insight to those who benefit from their expertise. In this way, they have "been there, done that." They'll use their wisdom to provide paths to success and steer people away from making moves that will likely end in turning a difficult situation worse or even catastrophic.

When you're facing a major obstacle or adversary, some battles are worth fighting, some require a strategy you haven't considered, and others require inaction. Mentors or coaches will dig into their past to help you determine the best course of action.

There is no finish line for mentors or coaches to cross that indicates growth is no longer necessary. Rather than view their role as something to look forward to retiring from, mentors and coaches are excited about growth in their own lives. They enjoy inspiring others to be equally as passionate about lifelong growth as well.

Creating or recreating oneself intentionally and skillfully isn't easy; mentors have done this over and over throughout their careers. They accomplished this through relying on a strong sense of self, flexibility, and agility that adjusts to many and often unpredictable sharp turns that are part of the fast-moving, complex, and often ambiguous world in which we live and work. They recognize the need to give back as an expression of gratitude for what they've accomplished, acknowledging that they too have benefited from the experience of others. As selfless sages eager to help you throughout your journey, they are interested in your success and experience deep satisfaction sharing in your results.

For these reasons, mentors and coaches are extremely valuable. Thus, a Leader will benefit from working with one or both. Mentors and coaches have reached this point in their lives through serious growth and commitment and expect the same from those with whom they work. They seek to be of service to those who are energetic, think deeply, and are practical about designing a path for themselves that aligns with their ambitious aspirations.

The Club

The writer Richard Bach said, "What the caterpillar calls the end of the world, the master calls a butterfly."[1]

The nature of being a Leader means you are taking the road less traveled where few will join you. At times you are charged with favoring one person or his or her position on something, which requires you to deny what another person wants. You must be cordial to those who mistreat you. You must often be more concerned about the well-being of people you supervise than they are of you. You must sweat out the details, while everyone else is free to ignore them.

Being lonely at the top means you are often responsible to make an unpopular decision that may leave others not understanding your motives. In this case, you often become the target of detractors and sometimes enemies that may question and even undermine your credibility. As a result, you may be the recipient of their attacks. CEOs, for example, must maintain a broad vision of their organization and the environment under which it runs. Sometimes, it is counterproductive or even unprofessional to reveal the background details behind why they chose one option over another.

CEOs must think of a future that is one, two, three, five, or even ten years out. Meanwhile, those who are mainly responsible to deal with the day-to-day duties of an organization lack the ability or the need to make decisions that will have long-term consequences.

It is often lonely when Leaders are by themselves considering the options in front of them and knowing that the success of their decision will be credited to everyone. Meanwhile, a Leader will be the primary person—often the only one—to be blamed for failure. It is also lonely when Leaders must smile, act as if they don't have a care in the world, and

1 Richard Bach, *Illusions: The Adventures of a Reluctant Messiah* (New York: Random House, 1977).

maintain a calm expression as harsh words and insults are hurled at them through direct contact with people and through news and social media.

Last, it is lonely making a decision that will affect the well-being of all stakeholders knowing that few would ever consider taking such risk. Whether you have a positive or negative worldview, the loneliness factor for leaders is usually the same. It's part of what you sign up for when you are the sole person to take responsibility.

Enter the club—where real power, recognition, favored lifestyle, desirable compensation packages, and prestige appear to reside. Along with the sacrifice required to reach the heights of positional leadership comes reward.

Within the club, Leaders connect with others at the top who have succeeded in attaining their chosen lifestyle. Rather than allowing obstacles and setbacks to keep them from high achievement, they have reached their biggest personal goals. Some may be living in their dream home, others may have a three-day workweek, while some are focused on philanthropy.

Whatever their original motives, they have realized the lives they envisioned for themselves, rather than have external circumstances determine their future. This type of organization used to be called the "old boys' club" or the "old-boy network" because it comprised only men who were heads of powerful organizations. Small towns had their old boys' clubs, and big cities had theirs.

While the size and scale were different for both, the concept was the same: It was a networking group for powerful men who ran the show in their communities.

Every profession and organization has its Leaders. They are key players across industries, and their decisions make history, cause fortunes to grow and shrink, and have wide-reaching implications. They are all part of an environment that dictates the lives of the often-powerless people around them. The club has provided camaraderie where there would otherwise be none. Being lonely at the top means Leaders have few networking options, and the club has provided them an opportunity to join others who were charged with shaping the reality of the masses.

Leaders have traveled the rocky road to high accomplishment, which has given them entry into the club. Its existence is not without controversy. They're often portrayed as secret societies of the rich and powerful. The very idea of an organization consisting of captains of industry and the livelihood of so many resting in the hands of the few is offensive to many and runs counter to a democratic vision of fairness, equality, and how society should work.

In the past, the organizations many Leaders ran had trade secrets and connections that gave them an upper hand when it came to investing and manufacturing. The club's controversial underpinnings are one reason its members maintain a low-key presence.

The club still exists today, but its makeup has changed dramatically. As society has evolved, the old-boy network is falling out of favor and becoming less relevant. Women and men of all stripes have risen in positional leadership, and this diversity is reflected in the updated version of the club. Today, members are subject to the influence of social media and its prominence in the public dialogue. The club must answer to the voice of the community at large and public opinion in a way that wasn't previously the case. Leaders are held to a higher degree of accountability in all facets of their lives, and club membership is no exception to this.

Being a club member is comforting and fulfilling. Playing first string is downright fun. The club fills one's need to meet and work with like-minded people where professional and personal sharing can take place.

Although your club colleagues represent different economic sectors, you share common challenges and concerns, and being able to express these to each other is satisfying. Club members respect one another's intellect and the causes they support. While some have gained their place through legacy, the vast majority have been invited to be a part of it through hard work and individual achievement.

The battles Leaders have fought on behalf of their respective organizations and against their adversaries are similar. Thus, inherent trust and loyalty exist in the relationships within the club. Throughout their careers, Leaders have separated themselves from their peers through their expertise, accomplishment, dynamic vision, and ability to influence and engage others with wisdom and integrity. While the purpose of the club is far from new, it has adapted to changing times. It still provides a vibrant and vital place for great minds to come together, enjoy one another's company, challenge one another, and address the greatest problems facing their industries and society at-large today.

Continually Evaluating Your Return on Investment (ROI)

No worthwhile accomplishment comes easily. Aspiring leaders will always pay a price as they climb their way to the top. And once they accomplish what they set out to do, they continually invest in their growth in order to stay competitive. Otherwise, they will find themselves losing ground to those who never stop improving. Continual growth propels Leaders forward on their journey as it unfolds before them.

Leaders are challenged to be both forward thinking and backward reflecting. Looking back may seem less important than looking forward. But all successful people need to take a bird's-eye view of life from beginning to end. By doing so, they'll be able to judge the successes and failures of their personal lives and careers.

The challenge for high-achieving and successful men and women is finding the time for this important process of personal reflection. They are fully engaged with the tasks unfolding before them in the present. While it is critical to focus on the end value of their investment of time and effort, it would be a glaring error to stop there. Leaders also examine whether the life they have created for themselves has resulted in joy and a feeling of accomplishment. Otherwise, despite a long list of achievements, Leaders may find themselves disappointed as they get overwhelmed by lesser issues—the little, annoying problems they encounter each day. Or they may have lost their momentum and dazzling performance of the past as they settled into the status quo.

Once you've realized your most ambitious goals, reflect on your past and ask yourself the following questions:

- Did the time, energy, and sacrifice create the outcome I expected and was it worthwhile?
- Did my personal and professional plans meet my expectations and did they leave me satisfied with my job?
- Did the passion and the commitment I invested in my initial investment lead to a payoff I'm satisfied with that includes my future filled with promise and hope?

These questions are a path to determining the return on investment (ROI) for goal accomplishment. In addition, young Leaders in particular may ask themselves:

- Am I happy?
- Am I respected?
- Have I reached the position in my field I was originally seeking, and do others see me as a leader?

Because young Leaders are still at the beginning of their professional path, most need a means by which to evaluate their initial progress and measure their team's performance. This includes identifying what they have accomplished so far and what work lies ahead. The best course for young executives is to include an ROI metric in their overall plan. Working toward a specific end increases the probability of successfully experiencing rewarding and desirable outcomes.

Answering yes to all these questions translates to a high ROI. If a Leader answers no to any of these, he or she has the option to determine how to change course or accept the status quo, which means allowing time and events to dictate his or her future.

As the first question indicates, part of measuring your success is to reflect on the intense time and energy you committed to in the past. In so doing, you determine if you experienced the ROI you envisioned that motivated you to move ahead—taking the road less traveled—while you watched those around you pick an easier path. For instance, when you were starting in your career, you may have been working two jobs. Or you may have been attending classes while working full-time. Or you may have been doing the preceding *plus* raising a family.

Your answers to the questions above are always based on personal and individual criteria. In other words, there's a level of subjectivity that means there are multiple paths to high achievement, and only your honest responses—and not another person's analysis—can determine if your ROI has met your goals.

For example, Leaders may be experts in their field and may have always expected their work would have purpose and be centered within the life of a well-respected company. They may desire to work with people with similar values and skills. The prestige associated with their executive positions may be an important measure of accomplishment.

Meanwhile, other Leaders use financial compensation as one measure of achievement. Their financial status allows them to provide for their families in a manner that meets the personal goals they have set for themselves. They are consumers in a capitalist country and want to be in a place where they can buy what they need and want. Compensation and growth potential are key to motivating them to climb the success ladder. They determine the degree to which they have the freedom to choose the lifestyle they seek to lead.

Balance and Leadership

Finding balance in life does not come in a sudden flash of enlightenment. Most Leaders figure out what it means to them and execute balance as they mature and assume increasing responsibility. Each person has his or her own way to determine what balance looks like. Some may define it by the period served in a position, some by job satisfaction, and others by the time shared with family and friends. In other words, simply calculating the hours allocated to a certain activity or task is an overly simplistic metric. Determining balance is about quality over quantity. For Leaders, measuring their overall ROI is important and not easy because the lines between professional and personal are often blurred.

In large urban areas, for instance, young adult Leaders may meet their colleagues for drinks after work. Or fraternal groups with long histories, such as the Kiwanis, Rotary Club, Elks Club, Optimists, and elite networking groups, which I referred to previously as the club, combine personal and professional aspects.

In contrast, some Leaders address this potential overlap between the two by strictly dividing their professional and personal lives. The social aspect of their lives may be solely aligned with activities outside of work. For example, Leaders with families may coach or attend their children's sports. They may work out at the gym or participate in motorcycle riding, cycling, running, cooking clubs, reading groups, or political or philanthropic organizations. These are just a few of the many avocations people enjoy.

Finding balance requires Leaders to define what it means to them. The challenge Leaders have is that personal and professional commitments often compete rather than support one another. You may be a parent who has your daughter's soccer game at the same time as a professional networking event. You may have committed to a Saturday date night with your spouse, but a deadline looms that requires your attention that evening. Leaders have no standard path to take; thus, maintaining balance requires explicitly determining what *balance* means to each person. Defining *balance,* as well as healthy and enjoyable professional and personal pursuits, is an important part of how Leaders measure their overall ROI.

Leadership and Relationships

Relationships are central to personal and professional success in life. Leaders have invested many years to assume their place at the executive table, and they've done so during the stage of their lives when they are also growing their families and raising children. Taking on one of these enormous responsibilities—Leadership or parenthood—is difficult in and of itself. Doing both well requires tremendous organization and support. It is crucial to build a life where you surround yourself with people who have a positive life perspective that flows from them. Having close relationships like these does not happen by accident. From the start of your professional life, be honest, direct, and clear about who you are, what you seek to achieve, and who will form part of your close professional and personal inner circles.

When you set out to accomplish great things, your ambitious plans will affect those closest to you. It is important to identify what you will bring to a relationship and what it will bring to you.

In *Don Quixote,* Sancho, giving attribution to a Spanish proverb, says, "Tell me your company, and I will tell you what you are." You do not want to be bogged down by those who do not appreciate or understand your mission and, in fact, are burdened by their own self-limiting beliefs. Your time and energy are limited, and those not supporting your aim will sap you of both. And even more dangerously, they will divert you from the immense and steady focus that the Leadership journey requires.

A rewarding partnership is one of life's greatest gifts. The relationship Leaders have with their partners is one that will either stifle or support their careers. The intense nature of being a Leader means the influence of their significant others is either positive or negative. A neutral influence, for the most part, is not an option. One reason is that the Leadership path requires an extreme dedication of time and focus; there is no such thing as a half-hearted or moderate commitment. Thus, it often requires significant sacrifice on the part of each partner.

Healthy relationships require giving and taking. Certain phases of a person's life may require more of one versus the other. For instance, an aspiring Leader may be in the career-building and educational phase of his or her career, which would likely need support from the family.

Imagine that Laura is married with young children, working full-time, and attending graduate school. Her marriage will benefit when both she and her spouse understand and accept the little time Laura has outside of work and school.

There may be regular periods during this phase of Laura's life where she gives attention to her family. Broadly speaking, however, we can characterize this as a taking period for her regarding her relationship with her immediate family. Specifically, her spouse bears more of the child-rearing duties because of Laura's current career-building stage. This doesn't necessarily reflect selfishness on her part but, rather, indicates the nature of her present circumstances where her ability to maintain her Leadership and family duties is put to the test.

In some instances, both partners are Leaders. This presents an exceptional challenge to couples. As we have seen with countless celebrity marriages, their relationships can break apart when one spouse's career takes off while the other's flounders. The spouse who isn't in the spotlight as much may believe he or she is more deserving of it or simply resents witnessing it.

In Laura's case, at one point in her career, she will be a sought-after expert. She will speak in front of large audiences, attend high-profile events, and be the target of media scrutiny, as well as receive prestigious awards and recognition.

Meanwhile, her spouse may not enjoy and have anticipated the ramifications that come from being married to Laura. The evolution of Leaders means their spouses are in the tough position of having to join them on the dynamic and bumpy journey when this may not have been the vision they had for themselves or their families. Relationships take work and incur many pitfalls and obstacles. The Leadership journey adds another level of complexity to already complicated circumstances.

Laura's relationship will benefit when she and her spouse have a clear understanding of her ambitious goals. They both must realize the challenges, sacrifices, and full commitment required for Laura to stay on her Leadership path. If they do not, the relationship will suffer or her aspirations to become a Leader will be stifled or both.

Having a plan is part of the Leadership journey. And this also includes one for the Leader's personal life. When Leaders clearly articulate their plans to their partners, they demonstrate their commitment to their most important relationship. They are doing their part to communicate their limitations of both time and energy, as well as what they can contribute.

In addition to navigating the complexities of running a household, clear and regular communication between partners is key to balancing between work and relationships. This includes practical duties such as budgeting, meals, and childcare and abstract ones such as having mutual understanding and respect for each other's goals.

Beyond marriage and within all our relationships, we want those around us to share our dreams and aspirations. Life circumstances mean we cannot seal ourselves completely off from those who do not share our vision. In some instances, dissolving ties may be necessary, such as in the case of abusive family members. But if we decide to maintain relationships with people who do not have our values, we need to establish boundaries that allow us to maintain high achievement while respecting ourselves and those we care about.

Leading by Example

Regardless of the sector you represent, being a Leader means you're engaging in positive, productive work. You may have reached positional leadership or see it in your future. In either case, you have a clear vision, which sets you apart from non-Leaders.

While this does not make a Leader inherently better or worse than anyone else, it does demonstrate the amount of time and energy Leaders allocate to influence others and create high-impact change.

All of us have the option to create a clear and ambitious path for our future. But Leaders have taken their hopes and aspirations and have turned them into a realistic and practical plan they've put into practice.

From the start, they realized their approach to goal attainment makes them exceptional.

If you've embarked on this journey, this description resonates with you. At the same time, being a Leader means you're also humble, which compels you to respect those who have not traveled the same arduous course and made the same choices as you. There is and should be room for different perspectives.

For example, let's say you have hired Daniel to fill an entry-level position within your organization. While he is fully qualified to fulfill his role, he has never had a clearly articulated plan for himself, whether in his personal or professional life. We'll describe Daniel's path in life thus far as unstructured, which contrasts with the highly structured one of a Leader.

It would be unlikely that, suddenly, because Daniel works for you, he sees your structured path and aspires to one day be a Leader. In fact, he may not see the value in it and may not want it for himself, even if he was aware of the difference between you and him.

At the same time, because he is part of your organization, Daniel needs to be a contributing team member. Part of this requires Daniel to have a structured plan in place to demonstrate improvement and growth. Teaching a largely unstructured person the value of structure, when it comes to your organization, is both challenging and necessary. Being a Leader means you understand and even appreciate that not everyone seeks or sees value in what you've pursued and the structure you've embraced. Effectively working with Leaders and non-Leaders alike is part of a measure of your ability to lead.

Because you've benefited from your own carefully developed and implemented plan, you are able to support your team as a mentor and example for them to follow. Demonstrating to those around you that success requires them to take responsibility for their own life is part of a Leader's duty.

In order for the organization you lead to reach its ambitious goals, you need a team effort. To move from lowercase leader to uppercase Leader requires the support of a team comprising men and women who understand they are not victims of their own circumstances. Rather, they are fully capable of overcoming any personal obstacles that stifle their growth potential. Those who do not see this possibility in themselves are highly unlikely to change. Any effective guidance you give is limited by the low expectations they have for themselves. Their ability to contribute to your organization's growth is equally stifled.

On the other hand, when members of your team aspire to the same excellence they see in you, your example is a powerful growth catalyst. Your high achievement and expectations are contagious. You may require them to follow processes, procedures, and protocols. They understand these are for their own benefit. Your team realizes you're interested in supporting their own growth and have their best interest at heart.

A Leader's performance is often largely a result of the quality support he or she provides the team. Your organization's ability to achieve is often dependent on how you leverage its potential. While team members are responsible to put in the time and effort, your job is to understand your team's strengths and weaknesses. By doing so, you will be able to provide them the resources they need for their own continued improvement and development.

Summary

In generations past, CEOs were rarely public figures. The heads of large companies might have been famous within their industries, but most were not household names. This provided a degree of privacy that doesn't exist today and allowed organizations to make decisions free of public scrutiny that is common now.

Today's Leaders, including CEOs, are under the inescapable, watchful eye of social media. The extent of the visibility they face has no precedent in history. The confluence of the internet and the evolution of leadership has allowed us to study and observe leadership's present-day form.

Leadership with a capital *L* is rooted in both aspiring toward a positional definition and devoting time to being a Leader beyond a C-level job title. The power of technological platforms has given Leaders a voice beyond what was previously possible. More Leaders are mentors, philanthropists, authors, public speakers, and gurus than ever before. In order to fulfill different roles, they have mastered the art and science of Leadership and do so through having a support network. Similar to a concert pianist, prima ballerina, astronaut, or pro athlete, becoming a Leader requires immense energy, sacrifice, and stamina.

In the next chapter, you'll learn the eight internal practices all Leaders put into action.

Chapter 3

EIGHT NONNEGOTIABLE LEADERSHIP PRACTICES

If you don't have time to do it right, when will you have time to do it over?

—JOHN WOODEN

LIVING ON INSTANT ramen, working part-time washing dishes in a restaurant kitchen between classes, and then going home to hit the books seemed like a lifetime ago as Rick sat looking out the window. The Airbus was making its descent, and the city below came into clearer view as the plane dropped below the clouds.

His business class seat provided him a welcome break from the nonstop travel. Crisscrossing the country speaking at conferences was both invigorating and exhausting for the thirty-seven-year-old executive.

Rick had just participated in a three-day, global technology conference held annually. The major event drew top talent from around the world. Attendees exchanged ideas, presented cutting-edge IT developments, and debated the most pressing technological issues that will affect every sector of the economy of entire nations, as well as the lives of people across the planet. Reflecting on being one among the thousands of industry elites gathered at the event put a smile on his face. It was a tangible reward for the tough road he had traveled to reach this point in his career, and he was bullish about what the future had in store for him.

Based on the solicitations from headhunters filling his inbox and voicemail, Rick knew his expertise was in demand. But not long ago, Rick had merely dreamed of being sought-after for his experience and knowledge.

In college, he had turned down the seemingly nonstop invitations to party, take vacations, and socialize after class. Whenever he was tempted to veer away from his studies, he reminded himself of the short-term sacrifices he needed to make to reach his long-term goals.

Rick understood how fortunate he was that his parents helped him meet his college expenses. He knew his academic accomplishments were the best way to show his gratitude for what he was given. So he studied hard, earned good grades, and managed his time well.

After graduating and once he was in the workforce, Rick met and then married his soulmate. From early in their relationship, they both expressed a desire to raise a family. Now, with two children in the house, Rick felt busier and more overwhelmed than ever. School, vacations, sports, music lessons, and more filled his family calendar. Striking a work-life balance was stressful, but Rick wouldn't want his life to unfold any other way. While this was his chosen path, he knew it was the opposite of fulfilling for many, including his close friends.

Todd, his best buddy from college, often joked that Rick's life was too traditional, had too many commitments, and required too much hard work. "I could never be a suit like you," he often said. Todd had earned good but not outstanding grades and loved to party during his undergrad years. He never married and didn't want to, rejecting being tied down to a demanding career and family obligations. While they chose different ways to lead their lives, the two appreciated their differences and never judged each other.

In fact, Rick sometimes asked himself, "Were the sacrifices all worth it?"

No path is perfect, and he saw the advantages of Todd's decisions. Sometimes when he was burdened by his countless responsibilities, Rick too wished he could let them all go in an instant. He knew he had paid a price. But everyone does. Life is about tradeoffs. The cliché "no pain, no gain" describes the challenges and sacrifices we make to attain what we want in our personal and professional lives.

From his college years, Rick envisioned working alongside experts in his field. He valued being respected, ethical, and holding a prestigious position. He sought a financial compensation that would allow him to provide for his family, support the lifestyle and socioeconomic status that appealed to him, and have the freedom to buy what he wanted and needed.

Similar to Rick, you too may have asked yourself the question, "Were the sacrifices all worth it?"

Did the time, energy, and dollars result in a fulfilling outcome?

For Leaders, the answer is a resounding yes. While the journey to becoming a Leader is as diverse as each person who has reached this exceptional level of achievement, Leaders nonetheless share common experiences that have resulted in their success. They have immersed themselves in certain practices to the point of mastery.

These procedures are distilled to eight that are nonnegotiable if one aspires to Leadership. They are all part of a Leader's daily personal and professional habits. Neglecting to follow any of them can undo the previous time and energy you've allocated toward planning and preparing to reach your ambitious goals.

You may read some of the eight practices and believe you have mastered them already. Meanwhile, others may seem to require more attention on your part. This is normal. The eight do not develop at the same time, just as growth in our lives does not occur evenly because lessons come at different times and in various ways. But all should resonate with you and go to the very heart of the intentions you have for your future. They are:

1. Maintain a healthy approach to stress.
2. Be realistic.
3. Reject anything that does not support your goal.
4. Embrace opportunities.
5. Choose the best way, even though it may be the most difficult.
6. Put yourself in social environments that support your goals.
7. Know your framework.
8. Plan for the future.

When you first read the eight practices, they may seem like a simple checklist. But this is certainly not the case. These are deep, meaningful habits that Leaders have committed to following throughout their lives to ensure success in their careers. You see this level of dedication across multiple disciplines and throughout history.

Practice 1. Maintain a Healthy Approach to Stress

Think of someone you know who has experienced extreme bodily pain. Every step she takes demonstrates the anguish she's feeling. She is so focused on her pain that she is barely able, or not able at all, to maintain the mindset of a Leader. While not impossible, her current condition is far from optimal to take on the challenges of Leadership.

Positive, confident people have a charisma that is infectious. They attract like-minded individuals and inspire and motivate them. When you feel good, you're clearly in a better position to navigate through the twists and turns of your professional path versus someone who is perpetually grumpy and negative.

Today's Leaders are working under increasingly complex, changing, and high-stress circumstances. Thus, you need everything you can control working in your favor to harness the inner resources necessary to sustain Leadership.

When you're healthy, you're equipped to manage stressful situations. We define stress as feeling psychological or physical tension. It can arise from events or thoughts and can manifest in frustration, anger, nervousness, or a combination of the three. Stress is our body's negative reaction to challenges or demands we're confronted with.

We all know people who don't handle stress well. Even the simplest challenge overwhelms them—let alone complex ones such as balancing large budgets, managing a major crisis, meeting huge deadlines, and evaluating or hiring staff. They become overly anxious and may succumb to their fears. Their health problems may be legitimate. Thus, all reasonable people should maintain a healthy level of personal responsibility. This means they should actively endeavor to maintain healthy practices that support the requirements of their job.

People who habitually do not cope well with stress will inevitably descend into despair. Overwhelmed, they may fail to meet their responsibilities as a positional leader. When given the fight-or-flight choice, these individuals take the flight path. This can manifest as an inability to make wise decisions, a reluctance to assume responsibility, or generally volatile behavior. Their nervous states will influence those they are responsible to lead. When leaders are unclear and doubtful in their decision-making, their subordinates are equally unclear and doubtful in the actions they are expected to take.

At precisely the moment when an organization requires decision-making that is both bold and wise, a fearful leader will fail to provide either. Examples of how poor stress management manifests itself include road rage, unreasonable customers shouting at salespeople, and parents violently shaking their young children to reprimand them, even when the child is acting out of fatigue. When stress triggers people, they can react in erratic ways. Their emotional flare-ups can, like a pilot light that erupts into a four-alarm fire, set ablaze in seconds work that took years to accomplish.

Positional leaders that succumb to stress rather than perform well under it manifest their triggered states in ways that you have probably witnessed or been the target of firsthand—no one likes being in the line of fire of an angry person.

They may react by being rude or disrespectful to their subordinates. Their objectivity may be hijacked to the point of harming the organization. For example, they may refuse to change direction from an otherwise unwise course of action because they are overly concerned about how others will perceive them. Or they may fear an admission of guilt could be a sign of incompetence or changing course could demonstrate weakness.

On the other hand, Leaders maintain self-control under difficult circumstances. By maintaining self-control, they view a situation with objectivity and clarity, thereby avoiding irrational decision-making that can have negative consequences, including permanently harming a project or, often even worse, losing respect and trust from those around them.

Whereas others may do their utmost to evade responsibility when triggered, Leaders accept it and remain calm, which gives them the ability to see possibilities and options when adversity strikes. In fact, the ability to perform well under pressure is one of the hallmarks of Leadership.

While Leaders would prefer to be mentally and physical healthy, the states of our minds and bodies aren't always within our control. We can succumb to ailments that affect our physical or cognitive function or both. Even those who take care of themselves can get sick. And chronic conditions can be debilitating.

Leaders may be struck down in their careers for problems out of their control at any point—they could be just starting out or in the midst of one of the highest points they'll ever achieve. And even those who experience decades of good health must plan for the inevitable reality of the aging process.

Rising to the demands of Leadership is difficult enough when circumstances are working in your favor. Add situations brought on by the frailty of life, and those former challenges that seemed relatively easy become arduous, if not impossible. Often, it is when we run the risk of losing our physical or mental strength that we realize we have taken our former abilities for granted.

Leaders at the beginning of their journeys benefit from taking a long-term view. For younger Leaders, seeing themselves ten, twenty, thirty, or more years into their careers may be difficult to imagine, but the far-off future is important to consider in the present. Being confronted by illness or other adversity is not the best time to decide to implement healthy habits.

Unfortunately, by this point any efforts you put forth may offer less relief than would otherwise be the case or make no difference at all. While sickness and disease have a genetic component, the healthy habits we follow for years and decades can prevent the onset of our predisposed conditions that could cut short our careers. In fact, all of us will have to face poor health at one point in our lives, but many debilitating conditions are avoidable or treatable through consistent self-care.

Good nutrition, healthy personal and professional relationships, taking moments for reflection, peace, and serenity, and a focus on continual improvement and growth are not goals you should wait for when the conditions are right and you have the time. Rather, they are part of your present life or what you actively work toward in the near-term.

Fostering and nurturing your well-being and health on a regular basis are essential for your path to long-term high achievement. Regardless of how hard Leaders are struck with sickness, they are still responsible to instill and model harmony within their organizations.

Challenges Leaders face to their well-being can push them toward even higher achievement or despair with little room for an in-between response. Difficult life circumstances often leave us with no option other than to pick an extreme side.

If Leaders are able to choose the path of hyperachievement when faced with extreme adversity, they will grow stronger and open themselves up to having more empathy and thereby being more appreciative of others' struggles. Or if a leader picks the path of resignation, he or she will most likely fall from the heights of hyperaccomplishment.

Throughout history, there are countless examples of people who have become disabled or come down with a severe chronic illness, and despite these otherwise debilitating setbacks, they are unstoppable and remain steadfast in how they live and what they do. They leverage the discipline and self-control they've developed over their lives to overcome adversity and continue to lead productive and useful lives, thereby further differentiating themselves from those who are self-serving, fail to appreciate the gift of life, or are unable to rise to the level of Leadership.

While Leaders may never be pushed to these extremes, part of planning the course of a person's career includes considering unfortunate scenarios that will affect his or her mental or physical well-being.

When pushed to our limits, we all benefit from having a plan in place. In addition, such regular planning is a reminder of both the innumerable factors outside our control and the importance of focusing and investing in improving what we can control. In terms of our health, this means placing top priority on taking care of our minds and bodies and doing so consistently.

Practice 2. Be Realistic

Back before famous men and women were household names, what if these exceptional people had been told, "You need to be realistic"? This would have likely been a critique of their supposedly impractical view of themselves, the world, and the potential within them.

But what does realistic mean? If the *real* in realistic when it comes to one's work is referring to a professional path taken that provides a nearly guaranteed outcome, then realistic is about seeking comfort and security and following a traditional plan. By being realistic according to this definition, the world's most famous and respected risk-takers would have never pushed themselves to accomplish greatness. In other words, "being realistic" could be the opposite of what it means to be a Leader.

A dream or a vision of something that breaks from conventional wisdom could certainly fall under the definition of unrealistic, that is, until hard work, focus, careful planning, risk-taking, and luck turn what was labeled unrealistic into the real.

By being realistic, Elon Musk would have never launched an all-electric car company that would compete with the world's biggest automobile manufacturers, and Tina Turner would have never gone beyond her humble beginnings to become the Queen of Rock and Roll.

Regarding luck, it is certainly an ingredient that many of the most successful people in the world say played a role in their lives: The weather was just right for a specific scientific experiment, the investor just happened to be available to meet with an entrepreneur, the economic conditions were ripe for a particular innovation, and more. But please don't count on luck . . . that would be a huge mistake because luck is a factor out of your control.

For every A-list Hollywood actor, there are countless men and women who sold all their possessions, packed up and moved to Tinseltown hoping for the best, and wound up unable to move beyond entry-level work in the hospitality industry. Waiting for luck will keep you from focusing on what is in your hands, which is prudent planning and maintaining a mindset rooted in reason, pragmatism, and audacity.

Consider a different take on being realistic. For me, it means having an honest view of constraints and possibilities regarding one's vision for his or her professional journey.

According to this definition of being realistic, you can dream big because, rather than being the main or only factor, dreaming is one aspect of your overall strategy.

Being realistic means setting ambitious and attainable goals as well as anticipating obstacles on the way toward reaching them. By maintaining agility and fluidity, Leaders adjust to evolving circumstances. For businesses, this means monitoring and then adjusting to changing market conditions. Because setbacks are to be expected, they will not come as a surprise. Rather, a plan is in place to adapt to new circumstances with as little disruption as possible and to realign goals if necessary. When confronted with adversity, being realistic gives Leaders the power to advance, rather than retreat.

Being realistic also requires separating prohibitive constraints from what are temporary setbacks. One common obstacle is money. Having ambitious goals often requires upfront financial investment. While this isn't always the case—with diligence and research you can often find ways to reduce costs—spending money, and lots of it, are nonnegotiable in some instances.

For business owners, the return for their startup investment comes from money credited or returned to the shareholder or investor based on earnings from interest or dividends. Being realistic means performing a diligent and objective cost-benefit analysis of the initial investment.

What Leaders do with income generated from a successful endeavor is one form of their return on investment. Examples of such ROI include a dream home, a lifestyle they envisioned for themselves, other material rewards such as boats, aircraft, and cars, personal-development support through psychotherapy or coaching, philanthropy, a legacy, and traveling.

Next, certain professions have high up-front costs. Becoming a lawyer, doctor, professor, certified public accountant (CPA), or certified financial analyst requires expensive post-graduate education and exams. If you can't completely self-fund your endeavor, making wise financial decisions requires fully assessing the resources you have, how long they will last, and the return on the startup phase of your investment. Perhaps after your investigation, you realize you qualify for scholarships or loans or you have time to earn money while you go to school. Today, many employers subsidize study if you commit to use your degree or certificate within the organization after you earn it. You'll see this with law degrees, MBAs, and public education.

If you can justify that the financial commitment, such as a student loan, is necessary in order to continue on your Leadership journey, then *how* you psychologically frame the fiscal constraint shifts. Rather than believing it's a barrier you cannot cross, you will work diligently to figure out how to overcome this obstacle.

Another common constraint is geography. To continue growing as a Leader may require you to relocate. Your expertise may be needed to fill a void away from where you currently work. Or perhaps the epicenter of your field is in another part of the country, and to further develop your expertise, you need to consider moving. An epicenter could also be where positions and mentors relating to your expertise are plentiful and you can advance in authority and compensation.

Relocation is normal for the top in their fields: Academics move to where the teaching positions are, scientists follow where the cutting-edge research in their field is taking place, technology entrepreneurs move to the Silicon Valley in search of venture capital, and actors go to Hollywood.

The deeper and wider your local close personal relationships are, the more the prospect of moving to another city, state, or even country may seem like a mountain you are unable to climb. Leaving the familiar—home, family, friends, the comforts of a community, and business relationships—may be too much of a sacrifice, but if you stay put, you may stop advancing in your career. Today, many on the lower rungs of the ladder find they can overcome this obstacle by working remotely. As the lockdowns starting in 2020 showed, technology offers many options to address this dilemma. But once you reach a certain level, relocation is usually the only option for advancement.

If a move is necessary to advance, then you must first thoroughly assess the situation on your own. Snap decisions, while easy and often feel good at the moment they're made, may result in later regret. To avoid this, perform an analysis using multiple assessments. Conduct thorough research, design and develop your plan, and use a variety of decision-making tools.

Many resort to a simple pros and cons list. While it may have its place in planning, be sure to understand its limitations when performing this exercise. The main weakness of a traditional pros and cons list is it requires simple yes and no responses. The Leadership journey is far too complex, and the choices you are presented with are complicated. A list that requires you to divide between yes or no neglects to address the nuances of difficult decisions, such as the maybes and what-ifs.

The best solutions and answers to life's difficulties often emerge from the most unexpected places. They may spring forth from unfettered creativity open to multiple possibilities and approaches—even ones that may initially seem absurd, outlandish, or unrealistic.

If the end goal of taking one approach versus another is the same, a strategy that emerges from a more innovative process could be less costly, more efficient, or profitable. If pros and cons lists are black and white and the best solution for your problem is gray, then it could be easily overlooked. You may be reducing or even prohibiting the possibility of coming up with new and supremely effective radical answers.

Rather than creating a pros and cons list, consider performing a ranking. Once you have identified your goal and explored a variety of ways to accomplish it, then add the following analytical step: On a scale of 1 through 10, rank each possibility. Doing so gives room for more nuances and sophisticated decision-making. It encourages you to come up with viable alternatives.

A critical aspect of creative planning should also include the Plan B approach. Assume you will hit obstacles, create in advance a Plan B, and then implement it when necessary.

How can you circumvent an obstacle that may deter you from achieving your goal? The possibilities are infinite. Do not limit yourself in the beginning; rather, explore all options. This includes the practical paths, as well as those others may consider unrealistic.

When you are overwhelmed with the prospect of overcoming a seemingly insurmountable obstacle, remind yourself that most constraints are simply problems seeking a solution. Thus, before attempting to figure out how to address a barrier, be sure you have a clear goal in mind.

Imagine James has a job interview. Prior to his meeting, he prepared answers to standard inquiries he anticipated, such as "Why do you think you're qualified?" and "What interests you in the position?" Unfortunately for him, his potential boss threw him a curve ball when she asked, "What's your goal and plan for your career?" Unprepared, he found himself bumbling his reply.

Despite this misstep, James was hired. But he never bothered to think more about this deeper question his boss had asked him. Two years into his career, he was confronted with an upheaval in his industry that resulted in his untimely layoff; the division of the company he was working for was sold off, and his position was cut because of the new merger. Without a clearly articulated goal, he experienced a professional crisis with no clear and ultimately satisfying way forward.

Had he previously developed a clear goal, the challenge of dealing with the layoff would have been mitigated. Knowing what he ultimately wanted, he would have been open to circumstances that presented themselves, as well as actively seeking the next step to meeting his ultimate objective.

Similarly, your goal sheds light on your circumstances and options. For business leaders, these can be factors in and outside their organization. Internal factors include budget and personnel constraints and the dynamics within the corporation or family business. External factors include federal and state regulations and other outside forces imposing their agenda that will affect your business. By focusing on goals, Leaders can discern whether a potential opportunity or solution should be pursued. This could require creating a new goal and discarding the old one altogether.

When confronted with a major obstacle that requires resolution, having a clear and well-thought-out objective is the most difficult part of the process—the rest is just hard work. Without being able to clearly articulate your goal, you're faced with tremendous ambiguity that significantly diminishes the likelihood of coming up with effective solutions to take you where you want to go.

Let's say you want to be a CPA. Although you are at ease with numbers, you don't understand financial terms in business, what is included on financial statements, or tax law.

But given your goal (to become a CPA), you can identify the skills you lack and what you need to do to acquire them. Now that you have this information, you can ask yourself if the time and financial investment required to meet your goal will provide you an ROI—both in regard to income with a new career and personal satisfaction.

All highly skilled forms of work require mastery in a particular knowledge set, and if gaining mastery poses an extremely difficult challenge, then one must seriously bear this in mind when planning. Working daily with serious constraints may result in dissatisfaction with the overall career path one has chosen. For example, if an aspiring actor stutters or a budding leader abhors speaking before large groups, each must be realistic by considering that limitation.

Fear is a natural response to taking risk. Dealing with fear requires first assessing if it is rooted in reality or is groundless. Some fears are worth heeding. They may indicate you need to reconsider your entire current course or simply part of it. Others are not worthy of your time and, in fact, are a waste of it.

If the fear is surmountable and worth confronting, you continue a realistic analysis and appraise the path required to accomplish your ambitious goals. What must you do to overcome this fear? If you allow it to veer you off course, you will inevitably fail. To succeed, you must devise a plan for getting past it. With practice and successfully confronting it, fear can be overcome.

Because you are realistic about it, you won't be caught by surprise when it comes up and will instead conquer it. While fear is a natural aspect of the Leadership path, when you are realistic about it, you'll be ready to evaluate its merit and make the course corrections necessary to continue forward toward reaching your goals.

Practice 3. Reject Anything That Does Not Support Your Goal

As Leaders progress, time becomes scarcer and responsibilities increase. Separating what contributes to your career advancement—while balancing your other primary goals, such as maintaining a solid family relationship—from what distracts from it becomes critical to your success.

Just as emerging Leaders are showing promise and making progress, they will be inevitably confronted with distractions. For example, a C-level position arises and offers excellent compensation. On the one hand, this seems like the perfect opportunity. But upon deeper investigation, accepting the offer may not align with a Leader's long-term objectives. Determining whether a new opportunity is one that should be embraced or rejected is often far from a black-or-white decision.

Next, personal relationships present a series of opportunities, as well as distractions. A relationship may arise when you least expect it. A new partner can offer comfort, companionship, and joy at a time when you could benefit from all three. Incorporating this important person in your life may be of great benefit to both of you if this person understands, accepts, and supports your long-term goals.

From marriage to job relocation, part of determining whether an activity is worth pursuing or is a distraction depends upon its return on investment. Monitoring and measuring are key factors in evaluating an ROI. Both offer statistical feedback. They provide Leaders with a clear path to assess whether the ROI aligns with their goals. At the same time, an ROI is not fixed.

A positive ROI is the benefit or value a person or organization experiences or will experience from a specified set of actions over a determined set of time. Examples include severance and buyout packages, a Leader's high performance including the quality of his or her work, the opportunities for future growth, and academic degrees. The latter—one you already have or one you are considering pursuing—may have a high ROI if it results in new opportunities or job security. Not all ROIs are tangible. Some less concrete ones, such as awards, honors, and praise, add to a Leader's satisfaction and well-being.

Practice 4. Embrace Opportunities

Where others see the mundane and ordinary, Leaders uncover wonderment and possibility. When Leaders gather, they embrace the opportunity to be among their fellow outliers, men and women who have spotted opportunity and potential through their watchful eyes and insatiable hunger to solve great problems.

Throughout a Leader's career, he or she will need to regularly course correct, sometimes in rapid-fire succession and other times gradually. Adjusting to change requires embracing rather than rejecting it and realizing that disruption, occasional failure, and setbacks are part of a Leader's path. The need to adapt is often an opportunity to reinvent oneself for the better. Embracing opportunities is not always a tangible action that can easily be observed and measured. Sometimes, it is an attitude or reflection of possibilities that may include the input of colleagues, mentors, friends, and family members.

A Leader's career may be defined by a breakthrough, such as a film director's masterpiece, a scientist's revolutionary invention, or an entrepreneur's cutting-edge business model. Broadly speaking, however, any accomplishment is primarily the result and part of a process, which can be characterized as a relentless drive to achieve to an extraordinary degree and doing so through teamwork.

Although significant pursuits separate a Leader from others, this version of success is not always associated with the traditional markers of high achievement, which are defined by academic degrees, licenses, and certificates. While these require discipline, intelligence, and focus to obtain, they do not guarantee professional success. If that were the case, all graduates from top universities would be Leaders.

Throughout history, Leaders with a wide range of education—from the most basic to advanced—have used their creativity, skill, and training in specific ways to bring about meaningful, worthwhile, and significant innovation.

Young Leaders with highly specialized education and training are embarking on their professional journeys at a remarkable point in human history. With the confluence of technology and global events, young Leaders are coming of age during a time unlike any other. Today's Leaders—courageous, smart, curious men and women who embrace opportunities—have the potential to solve problems of literally global importance to the future of human civilization.

Practice 5. Choose the Best Way, even though It May Be the Most Difficult

Any strategic plan has at least three basic points:

- Identify the overarching goal and evaluate its quality.
- Establish milestones along the way and evaluate each.
- Have a process for evaluating the outcome of the plan.

The first and most fundamental part is to identify the overarching goal and evaluate its quality. Identifying the goal means addressing where you plan to end up and the outcome you wish to achieve. "I want to be a CEO or a C-level executive" is an example. Next, your goal's quality addresses whether it is worth the immense time, energy, and risk required to attain it.

In the end, once you've reached your goal, those around you may perceive that your journey was easy and likely, given your focused personality. While a Leader's poise and confidence may indicate his or her journey has been smooth and predictable, Leaders are fully aware of the dangerous waters they've confronted as well as the risks they have taken and will continue to take.

Regarding risk, the greater it is, the bigger the reward or failure. Abject failure is possible. Many of history's greatest Leaders failed repeatedly throughout their lives. In fact, Leaders often point to their mistakes as important indicators along their professional paths—sometimes they wear them as badges of honor. Others believe it is part of what makes goal attainment interesting. If accomplishment were like gambling in Las Vegas, working toward it might feel like putting all your chips on, say, 30 in roulette. A win means you've hit the jackpot. A loss means you're going home empty-handed.

Experiencing failure is not a requirement of the Leader's path. Making errors that could have been averted is not wise or heroic. In fact, with wisdom and prudence, Leaders can avoid such mistakes and arrive safely at their destination. But the possibility of failure is part of assessing risk as you proceed along your journey. Asking yourself if you can handle failure when it arises is a key consideration in evaluating the quality and value of your goal.

Each person has a different failure threshold. Being afraid of failure is not necessarily negative, and embracing it is not necessarily positive. But part of determining the quality and value of your goal is to consider what difficulty and sacrifice you are willing to endure, the amount of failure you can sustain, and how much you can afford to lose. For example, if you are married with three young kids and you are a caring breadwinner, you will assess failure differently than if you are young, single, and responsible to support only yourself.

The second part of a strategic plan is to establish milestones along the way and evaluate them, which includes identifying what support, financial and otherwise, you need to reach each. In the case of CEOs, they may implement a collaborative leadership model after realizing their organization will benefit from doing so. Shifting to this new approach will require them to determine the resources they'll need and then go about acquiring them.

The third part of your strategic plan is to have a process for evaluating what you accomplished—success, failure, or something in between. This means each part of your strategic plan has a clear value that is straightforward to measure. You and others are able to easily determine if you met your objective. Here, your biases are important to acknowledge. We all have them, and they are based on our past experiences. You want to make sure you're measuring your objectives in an impartial way.

One way to avoid falling prey to your biases is to have an outsider evaluate your progress. A third party, in other words, someone who is not influenced by your subjective perspective, will add credibility and integrity to evaluating your outcomes.

While you want to meet your goal and milestones, missing the mark is part of the Leadership journey. It is far better to know you're off course than to succumb to your biases and fears, thereby refusing to acknowledge you need to change your strategy or drop it altogether. Deviating from your objectives is inevitable.

You may have decided to structure your organization a certain way. Over time or suddenly, broader economic conditions change, and the approach that once worked no longer does. Or your choice may have resulted in poor outcomes—being a Leader means you still make mistakes. The key is to identify your misstep as quickly as possible and have a means to skillfully course correct. This may require restructuring, redesigning, or recreating.

Navigating through change is an art form. And those who do it well embrace it. They plan carefully for the short and long term. They don't necessarily look for the hard path if a simpler route is superior. Many times, however, the road dotted with pitfalls offers the greatest reward. While there may be safer paths to travel and ones that many have already taken, embarking on the tough path often has the biggest impact and creates significant change. Taking the bold step of beginning this arduous journey is what separates Leaders from others.

Beyond the three basic points, your strategic plan is also influenced by your nature. This refers to your background, upbringing, life experience, and genetics. We are born into the world with specific characteristics and tendencies. The environment in which we are raised fosters and nurtures or rejects and stifles who we are. Self-awareness of your nature fuels one of the most fulfilling and important aspects of Leadership: enjoying the journey.

With self-awareness, many of our strengths and weaknesses can be improved upon, but it is also important to consider our predispositions. Some aspects of our personality clearly require our full attention. An extreme example of this is people succumbing to their addictions in their various forms. This frequently harms themselves and those around them. Meanwhile, other aspects of our personality are less easy to identify as requiring change. In these instances, there is no one formula to follow. Rather, we can tap into multiple external and internal resources.

External examples include coaches, consultants, therapists, colleagues, and family members. A Leader's gut instinct is often his or her best internal guide. Some of the soundest advice we receive comes from within ourselves. Many of us can investigate our past and pinpoint a moment in our lives where we were presented with a decision that had far-reaching consequences—good or bad.

The silent voice inside us told us to decide yes or no, and in no uncertain terms, the answer was clear. We either listened to this internal wisdom or rejected it. As a result, we lived the consequence of our decision. We recall this as a pivotal event that shaped the course of our lives.

This is where spending time in silence, peace, and reflection is important. While on the surface time may seem better spent elsewhere, increasing our self-awareness improves our decision-making and provides us with the mental breaks we need to maintain long-term high performance. We may be taking a walk outside, and suddenly a solution emerges to a problem we weren't able to figure out. We also gain clarity and shed light on our personalities when we self-reflect. We may be aware that we are risk averse to the core. Through listening to our hearts, we can determine whether the challenge we face requires us to overcome our risk aversion or to search for alternative courses of action, ones that flow with our safety-seeking tendency rather than fight against it.

There are moments in our lives when we benefit from putting aside our fears and charging fully ahead. Meanwhile, other times, listening to our fears prevents us from taking foolish action. The wise path is often the difficult one. It requires being curious and open-minded and taking risk while thinking and planning.

Most working adults do their jobs out of habit and necessity. Showing up to work is an obligation rather than a preference. They postpone many of the things they want to do in life, waiting until retirement when their work commitments will no longer impede their aspirations. But Leaders refuse to defer fulfillment.

They have pictured their career path from the start and experience immense satisfaction from realizing their vision. A Leader's nature is high energy and focused. While they have long-term goals they work toward, they don't postpone satisfaction to a later date. They are always tapping into their creativity and having fun solving complex problems. Leaders strike the difficult balance between being patient as they work toward a future goal and embracing the present and all it has to offer.

Practice 6. Put Yourself in Social Environments That Support Your Goals

We are social creatures, designed to interact with others. While we have a propensity to socialize, humans have a wide range of how this manifests. On the socializing spectrum, the extremes on both ends are extroverts and introverts. We all know enormously extroverted individuals who, throughout most of their waking hours, prefer to be surrounded by people. On the other end are highly introverted men and women. Their tendency is to seek quiet and solitude. Most of us, however, have aspects of both.

Given our nature to be social beings, we must take seriously those we choose to surround ourselves with. Young people have less say in the matter. Although they can select their friends outside of their homes, they can't choose their families. And the influence parents have on us is clear when we look at the lives of young people.

Most children become adults who follow in the footsteps of the general family patterns their parents modeled for them, as well as fall under societal conditioning. Religion, political beliefs, dietary preferences, and child-rearing standards are all passed from parent to child. Children absorb their family experiences—both positive and negative—through osmosis. Childhood abuse, addiction, and poverty can result in trauma so significant that cycles repeat, often unconsciously.

In generations past in the United States, and still today in some families here and cultures throughout the world, daughters live with their parents until they marry, and college is not an option. For a young woman raised under such a setting, to break from family tradition is both uncommon and usually comes at great risk.

Moving away from family patterns and societal conditioning typically requires intentional effort. The immense internal drive required to reject one's upbringing and take a different course demonstrates the power of our environments over our lives.

Amanda was an example of this. She was a high school student when I met her. During her senior year, she reached a major life crossroads. Her parents were Mexican immigrants, and she grew up in a working-class neighborhood in Southern California. The urban high school she attended had a dedicated staff that created a program for high-achieving students from challenging backgrounds. When Amanda graduated, she was the first in her family to earn a high school diploma.

While this was a milestone and a proud moment for her parents and her boyfriend, none of them valued education as highly as she did. Her parents worked hard and had created their own version of the American Dream by establishing a small restaurant. Just as her siblings had done, Amanda was expected to work full-time in it now that she had finished school. Her twenty-three-year-old boyfriend agreed with this plan. He too had immediately worked full-time in the service industry after high school and didn't go on to college.

But thanks to Amanda's innate drive and a powerful mentorship program in her high school, she planned to attend a university. Unfortunately, given the obstacles those closest to her presented, the likelihood of being the first college graduate in her family decreased significantly.

For Amanda to move beyond the established norm in her world would require her to go against the wishes of the most important people in her life. Work in the family business, marriage in her early twenties, and children soon after were the main highlights of her family's trajectory for their daughter's life. Unfortunately, college didn't fit within this path. If Amanda deviated from the plan they had for her, she feared they would interpret her actions as going against the values they represented and had instilled in her.

Her parents' objection could be based on practical considerations. Earning a university degree and joining the college-educated workforce was unimaginable to her parents, who had limited formal education. They had never been allowed on the white-collar highway and thus had no frame of reference of what that landscape looked like. Their reality was rooted in how the family business met their needs and would continue to do so. Under this paradigm, the money, time, and effort required to, first, apply to colleges; second, eventually earn a degree; and third, possibly be away from the family business were senseless obstacles and damaging to the family.

Meanwhile, thanks to Amanda's mentors, they gave her a glimpse of what the professional path looked like and the opportunities it would provide her, as well as the steps she needed to take to reach her goals.

Amanda did not think going to college would be a sign of disloyalty or betrayal to her family, but she was afraid they could interpret it that way. A Plan B would be for her to postpone her college ambitions and go to work right away. But she knew that going to school while maintaining family, romantic, and work responsibilities would present enormous barriers to earning a degree.

The status quo of her family dynamics dictated one set of actions. Meanwhile, Amanda's inner voice told her to reject what was deemed normal and acceptable within her family. Thanks to the seeds her mentors planted in her, she had a vision of what that future could hold. This drove her to break from her family expectations and pursue her own dreams. If marriage and children were part of her plans, she would need to extend her timeline for both to fit within her new path.

Amanda took the bold step of attending college after high school. Fortunately, while her parents didn't support her decision, they didn't fully object to it either. Her boyfriend, on the other hand, rejected her ambition. He interpreted it as excessive and unrealistic, and their relationship suffered. While the breakup was tough and gradual, once it was over, Amanda knew it was in her best interest and marked her new journey.

Tapping into her intelligence, confidence, and motivation and receiving the support of mentors who guided her, Amanda eventually earned her bachelor's degree. After graduating, she moved on to a lucrative and satisfying job.

Reaching her goals required sacrifice and withstanding her family's objections. She worked at the family restaurant while maintaining a full course load. Seeing her commitment to both her studies and family, they came to accept and be proud of her decision. In fact, seeing the tangible results of her unstoppable drive made them immensely proud of what their daughter had accomplished.

Amanda's example points to the importance of whom Leaders surround themselves with. The impact of those around them demonstrates the power of our environments, their influence over our lives, and the importance of the decisions we make. Breaking from negative patterns instilled from a young age is an enormous challenge.

Ideally, family and friends of Leaders care about them, understand their ambitious goals, and will support them on their journey. If these people don't, Leaders will benefit from seeking out individuals who will. It takes only a small group of like-minded and exceptional individuals to have a powerful impact on a Leader's life.

In Amanda's case, her small group of mentors offset her previous conditioning and inspired her to pursue a path beyond what was part of her family's reality. Similarly, men and women who understand a Leader's ambition play a role in his or her ability to push ahead.

Professionals in your workplace and school (when you're pursuing a graduate degree) can provide flexible work hours to accommodate your studies, financial aid to help cover educational costs, and mentorship.

When Leaders surround themselves with positive, ambitious individuals, they open themselves up to meet people who can provide the resources that can catapult them to new levels of accomplishment.

Countless teenage movies point to the influence of the bad crowd on good boys and girls. The innocent teen is offered drugs. He partakes, and his life spirals downward from there. The smart girl is teased constantly and seeks revenge on her bullies. While these movie tropes may seem isolated to impressionable adolescents, Leaders too are influenced by their environments, often in subtle ways, and they must never lose sight of this.

A less dangerous equivalent of hanging with a bad crowd for Leaders is when they surround themselves with good people who don't understand or are not willing to support them on their journeys. High achievement requires tremendous sacrifice, and those who don't share this level of motivation may hold Leaders back from pursuing their ambitious goals. High achievement and success involve personal choices Leaders must make with an understanding that only they can make these big decisions. Taking on this degree of personal responsibility requires understanding that no one else can force or require them to make a choice that isn't in a Leader's best interest. By setting exceptional standards for yourself, you increase the likelihood of reaching ambitious goals. Thus, surround yourself with individuals who are as positive, self-disciplined, and optimistic as you.

Practice 7. Know Your Framework

Your plan's foundation reflects who you are, which comprises your core beliefs, which is how you interpret the world. These beliefs are typically rigid and strongly held ideas that do not readily change. They include the values you hold true, as well as your beliefs about yourself, others, and the world. Core beliefs form the basis of your thoughts and actions. They provide answers to questions such as:

- Is the world harsh and cruel or generous and rewarding?
- Are people essentially good or bad?
- Do I tend to be brave or meek, fearless or fearful?
- Am I intuitive and thoughtful or spontaneous and direct?
- Do I believe women and men can deliver equally on a given project?

- Do I work mainly in order to gain compensation, or is purpose an important motivator?
- Am I a spendthrift, or do I place a high importance on saving?
- Am I conservative or progressive?
- Am I religious or nonreligious?
- Do I value the group or the individual?

There are pluses and minuses to many of the preceding core beliefs where one is not superior to the other. But this doesn't mean negative core beliefs are harmless. When leaders have core beliefs that characterize them as fearful or meek, they will struggle moving toward their goals with confidence. Leaders who view their world as harsh and cruel will have difficulty trusting and connecting with stakeholders who will help execute the strategic plan. These Leaders will benefit when stakeholders respect and admire them. Negative core beliefs hinder what you do and how you do it. These pose the greatest obstacle to those who are otherwise working hard to execute their plans.

Regardless of how impeccable the plan, if it does not align with your core beliefs, this will hinder its effectiveness. If you attempt to ignore relevant aspects of your character, this will reveal itself as your plan unfolds. Knowing your core beliefs plays an important role in your ability to maintain the sustained stamina necessary to pursue big goals.

Obstacles will impede your progress. Sometimes you'll move quickly through milestones, and other times you'll suffer long dry spells. When you face difficulties, such as periods where progress slows down or even stops or setbacks are pulling you backward, you may realize your tendency to self-doubt and question the validity of your efforts. An awareness of your core beliefs can allow you to act and look for the tools that will counteract any self-sabotaging thought patterns. As a result, you'll more likely successfully stick to your plan from which you'll experience positive outcomes.

The way you respond on a consistent basis to the issues your organization faces determines your ability to assume greater authority and responsibility. Knowing your core beliefs increases your ability to be a strong, steady Leader. From day one of launching a plan, Leaders realize it will require course correction. They will confront many issues. Even after they complete it, another plan will require their attention. A Leader establishes a plan, works toward it, reaches it, and establishes another. This endless cycle is part of the Leadership journey. Just as a person who pursues wisdom never stops when one insight emerges, Leaders see their plan as continuously taking them from one point to another.

Boldly executing an ambitious plan is full of risk. A plan without consideration of core beliefs rests on a crumbling foundation, one that will fall apart eventually. When Leaders use their core beliefs as part of their planning process, they create a strategy that reflects how they perceive and interpret the world. Such considerations give Leaders the information necessary to remove personal obstacles that would otherwise impede their progress, if not result in outright failure.

Often, students in academic leadership programs are assigned a straightforward task: Carefully consider and then write down your core beliefs and how these apply to your leadership philosophy. Your philosophy reflects what you want to achieve and how you plan to influence or lead others or improve the world. This one-page assignment pushes Leaders to analyze what makes them tick.

Years later, Leaders may reflect on what they wrote. Often, they make a minor revision or change a word that reflects their subsequent experience. But overall, a well-considered leadership philosophy, despite the passing of time, remains fairly consistent throughout a Leader's professional journey. With self-awareness leveraged early on, Leaders tap into invaluable insights that will empower them in their work. They are able to identify areas that demonstrate strength and areas of weakness that require growth.

Core beliefs are the starting point for us to build a world that feeds and supports our hopes, goals, and dreams. By knowing who we are, we are better equipped to navigate through our plans. When we hit roadblocks, we increase the likelihood we'll overcome them if we know our stress triggers.

Insight into our core beliefs increases our objectivity, which will enable us to adapt and see opportunity that we may otherwise overlook. A successfully executed plan provides an ROI, and as we work through it, our plan provides us with awareness of areas where we need to improve and grow. Knowing our core beliefs provides us with a depth of understanding that, when used effectively, guides the most important actions within our plans.

Practice 8. Plan for the Future

Soon after I founded my first organization, my board of directors approached me with a straightforward yet personally jarring request. They wanted me to create a training program that would enable a fluid leadership succession in the event I no longer served. This strategy would be based on a sound team of leaders throughout the organization that I was also charged to develop. At first, I was taken aback.

"I'm in the prime of my career, making great progress here, and years away from retirement, so what's the rush to replace me?" I thought to myself.

But upon further objective reflection, I realized the logic behind this request. All Leaders are sought-after, aggressively recruited, and sometimes poached from one company to another. Or they may have to leave their position abruptly for any number of other reasons. Thus my board of directors wanted to ensure a continuity of leadership in the event I left my post.

Having a succession plan is critical to all companies that strive to remain competitive over the long term. *Sustainability* is a term that describes this continuity of an organization's high-performing operations as it transitions from one leader to another. In my case, I initially felt threatened by my board of directors' request. I wondered if my board was already looking to replace me after serving as its leader for only a short time. Early on, I viewed the board's appeal as a tough pill to swallow. But experience later taught me to see it completely differently. The greatest compliment to a high-level Leader is that the organization can run well without him or her.

With the growth of our organization, I realized the importance and benefit to having a core group of Leaders trained and well equipped to act as my surrogates. Later, as they matured in their positions and expertise, I delegated more authority and responsibility to them. Although over time members of my team have come and gone, a culture emerged within the organization that strongly reflected our core values and practices. Through the years, I've trained and guided others in our highly effective approach.

As the leader of a large, vibrant organization, I had the benefit to always have eight or nine leadership team members that were tough, smart, and dependable. Any one of them had the capacity to step in as an excellent CEO.

In turn, the leadership team that headed different departments and divisions began to train and coach another cohort of positional Leaders who were also tough, smart, and dependable and continued to grow in expertise and experience. As the organization expanded, so did the need to have people that would support every aspect of its function.

To address our needs and adapt to our continued evolution, we developed a school focused not only on K through 12 pupils but also on another level of education that centered upon the growth and development of all employees; we call the program Altus University. Every person within the organization works directly to achieve our overarching strategic goals and annual work plans. All of them have access to and participate in Altus University. There is a minimum amount of time that every employee gives to Altus University, but most far exceed this. A similar means for training people to support the long-term needs of your organization is equally as priceless and important.

As our broad-based support for all employees generated enthusiasm and interest, we expanded the scope of our university. We added specialized trainings, introduced new technology updates on compliance, and provided opportunities for high-quality on-the-job training.

These offerings correlate directly to the product or main business associated with the work done in the organization. In regard to teacher training, we offer courses in curriculum, individualized and personalized instruction, and mental health support for students. Workshops include techniques for working with special needs students and collaboration with parents and community partners. Beyond improving performance within the organization, we also offer support for growth in health and nutrition, personal finance, retirement planning, and other areas that contribute to the workforce's well-being.

A few years ago, due to the success of Altus University, we created an extension to it; we call it the Fellows Program, and anyone within the organization may apply. It provides potential leaders the opportunity to work on a yearlong project that analyzes, reviews, and improves a process already in place within our organization or integrates an innovation that directly enhances its function.

A senior-leader mentor guides the fellows' work. The yearlong experience strengthens the fellows' connection to our everyday inner workings and operations. Participants are introduced to departments outside of those with which they are familiar. Their projects reveal for them how closely tied, integrated, and interdependent the departments are with each other. In turn, senior leaders can observe and identify potential candidates for future positional advancement. Some fellows may seem ready to step into new responsibilities, while others may benefit from a plan to further develop their skills in a specific area.

In this way, the Fellows Program creates a constant flow of skill and talent. Experienced leaders groom others using the Altus vision, mission, values, and goals as their guide. The Fellows Program further helps embed and perpetuate a culture continuously open to new thoughts, ideas, and practices.

The leadership team carefully considers applicants, evaluates their quality of work in their current positions, and considers the likelihood that the candidates have sufficient confidence, self-discipline, maturity, and drive to assume more and more responsibility within the organization.

We see Leadership as something practiced at each level and position within an organization. Because Leadership is a relationship, everyone must be prepared to operate as either a leader or a follower, depending on the situation. Although there are those that assume positional leadership, a well-designed succession plan has Leadership training at every level.

Our process engenders continual improvement that includes evaluations from workshop participants and always encourages suggestions for ways to better our programs.

Combined, Altus University and the Fellows Program are designed to, first and foremost, deliver the highest-quality academic program to students, improve the life of every employee, provide both students and staff with resources to overcome challenges and constraints, and help all succeed in and outside the school-workplace environment.

All organizations need a succession plan or a means for effectively transitioning authority or power from one group of individuals to another. These plans vary, based on the needs and structure of each company. Within a corporation, they often take the form of a policy that the board of directors develops and approves. The policy includes details outlining how the highest authority within the organization will be recruited and hired, a clear description of the protocols, and how they must be followed. For example, the policy may direct the board of directors to appoint a senior administrator (such as a vice president) as interim leader during the job-search process.

Within small, family-run businesses, a succession plan may be a document that outlines who should take charge of the company if the current leader is unable to do so and under what circumstances such a decision will be triggered. The current owner may be in charge of drafting this document and name a specific person such as a son, daughter, or spouse.

If children, spouses, or other family members are designated to take over, the assumption is that they have been fully prepared to do so when the time comes. Just dropping someone with little knowledge of how the business operates into the highest leadership position is unfair and puts the business's future at great risk. In fact, the succession plan's purpose is to prepare the next person in line to assume responsibility of the business and the well-being of its employees, who in many cases have committed years of hard work and played a fundamental role in the organization's growth and accomplishments.

Their dedication is invariably tied to their support of the organization. Thus, a transition is much smoother when the new CEO knows and values the organization's history and culture that lives and breathes within the people who do the daily work required for high achievement. For CEOs from the outside, such instruction will be especially important.

For a succession plan to succeed, a culture where daily training and coaching are embedded throughout the organization must be firmly established far before it is given the green light. No two people are alike, and no two leaders are the same either. But when the new executive's version of leadership aligns with the successful practices currently in place throughout the organization and he or she maintains them, this is a measure of a well-crafted and well-executed succession plan.

It is inevitable that new leaders bring with them a new leadership style. That said, one should be open to the fact that change will occur over time. The new CEO will incorporate his or her vision, ideas, and approach to how the work is done while also honoring the organization's history, culture, and purpose.

Summary

Tibetan Buddhist monks have spent their lifetimes mastering their contemplative skills. At first glance, introspection may seem simple—sitting quietly and observing one's thoughts. But through deeper investigation, you realize these masters have refined this general practice over the centuries to the point of identifying specific aspects of perception. They have developed techniques to guide other contemplatives to reach the same levels of mastery, thereby making their skills transferrable to others.

In this chapter, you've learned about techniques that result in Leadership mastery. While these eight practices are not designed to generate extraordinary mystical experiences, they do result in exceptional professional success. Similar to any aspect of our lives where we seek long-term benefit, we are fully engaged in these practices in a way that is as intentional as consistently going to the gym and maintaining a healthy diet. Anything less than full-fledged long-term commitment will not result in being a Leader.

Most of us do not aspire to being Tibetan meditation masters. But for those of us that seek to be Leaders, our dedication to fulfill our life's purpose will set us apart from those with merely hopeful intentions. By adhering to the eight practices, you are following a Leadership formula that will bring about success during these times of unprecedented change.

In the next chapter, we'll explore how creating a network of allies will propel you to Leadership excellence.

Chapter 4

GETTING PEOPLE ON YOUR SIDE, PART 1

The secret of change is to focus all of your energy not on fighting the old, but on building the new.
—**DAN MILLMAN**, *Way of the Peaceful Warrior*

AN EERIE QUIET was in the halls where, during school hours, the sound of a sea of students moving from one class to the next filled the now silent space. During passing periods, the high school hallways were as busy as an airport terminal. In this crowded place, teenagers expressed every emotion: happiness, sadness, anger, frustration, elation, and more.

For eight years, Bob had supervised this bustling space. Now, with students gone for the day and his retirement celebrations over, this would be his last time occupying the campus as its principal. As he reflected on his tenure, he was reminded of the countless hours he spent—long before the morning student rush and after the dismissal bell rang—leading an amazing group of teachers and providing students the best educational environment possible.

He felt a lump in this throat as he thought about the nights and weekends crammed with extracurricular activities such as Friday night football games, proms, musicals, plays, and community outreach. Whether Bob was participating in a Kiwanis meeting, watching a pep rally, training teachers, or speaking to reporters, he took pleasure in playing so many roles. Every day was different, and he enjoyed taking on new responsibilities. And as the school's leader, he recognized the importance of his position. Bob not only rose to the challenge but also appreciated that his role allowed him to instill his vision within the school culture.

Being the principal meant he was often the first one blamed for any outcomes that didn't meet expectations, and when there was a positive outcome, he routinely passed praise to others. Occupying his position was demanding, stressful, and often unpleasant. But being able to improve the lives of everyone who walked through the halls of his school far outshined any adversity he had to overcome.

Bob made his way down the still, dark hall and into his office. He had stripped the walls of framed degrees, artwork, and awards. His desk was cleared of photos, trophies, and his electronic devices. Most of his belongings occupied his car's back seat and trunk. One cardboard box remained on his desk, and with that carried out in his arms, his mark in the space would be erased. While he would no longer have a physical presence on campus, his legacy would carry on long after he retired. This meant his successor had inherited a plum position.

Rather than having to turn around an underperforming school, the new principal merely had to carry on the high-achieving culture his predecessor had established. In this regard, Bob envied how easy the principal's job would be. At the same time, he had to admit that he loved the thrill of making a weak school strong.

Retirement from being a principal didn't mean he was withdrawing from professional life. His next prestigious position was as an administrator in the district's central office. There his vision would spread beyond one school and extend to all of them.

Starting over, after eight years of being the top Leader at his school site, he would now be required to establish his credibility in a new setting. While he knew the employees in the central office, they weren't his everyday colleagues. He was entering a new work culture where he would need to earn the respect of his coworkers through his future performance. Although his reputation preceded him, in his new capacity, his colleagues would not allow him to coast on it.

On the one hand, Bob needed to earn the trust and confidence of the staff in the department he now headed. On the other hand, he was hired to improve its poor performance. Persuading, rather than creating opposition and hostility, would require masterful communication. Engendering a work culture that rejected the status quo and embraced his vision would require creating more advocates than adversaries.

To succeed under these difficult circumstances was one reason he was hired to fill his next post. His ability to turn a struggling school into an excellent one eight years ago convinced the hiring committee that he had what it took to improve the department he would head. Now it was up to him to prove them right. In order to achieve the outcomes expected of him, he referred to his high school playbook. Getting people on his side was at the top of his turnaround plan.

■ ■ ■

In its simplest form, leadership can be described as a relationship between leaders and their followers. Dig deeper, however, and you see the challenge Leaders face in making sure this relationship is effective and long lasting. They have the enormous responsibility to attract and hire the best people—men and women who will play a fundamental role in bringing about the Leader's specific purpose or cause. Jim Collins, author of *Good to Great,* famously told his readers, when looking to improve an organization, to first consider if they have the right people on the bus, as well as the wrong ones off it.

Attracting and hiring people who have a cursory and short-term interest in your project is far easier than finding individuals who will maintain the stamina necessary to reach major goals. A disciplined and strong work ethic is innate to those that represent your wise hiring decisions.

At the same time, you're also responsible to nurture and provide them the resources necessary to bring about the results you seek. In this regard, a leader's title means little. His or her name may appear in a position of authority on an organizational chart. But this title on paper does not assure that his or her subordinates assigned to a task will be devoted, be loyal, and commit themselves wholeheartedly to the project or the leader. So the question Leaders are charged to ask themselves is, "How do I get people on my side?" In this chapter, you'll learn how.

Actions Effective Leaders Take

A Leader's playbook for success is clear. His or her mission is to first create an open culture. Doing so requires accountability, honesty, and welcoming others to collaborate with you. By doing so, you show you have nothing to hide. When you invite collaboration, others will see how you think and work. Accountability means a willingness to take responsibility for one's action. You build credibility by upholding and modeling transparency and accountability. Both require vulnerability, which means Leaders subject themselves to praise or blame or both.

Before the Information Age, Leaders had a great deal of control over how they would maintain transparency and accountability. They were largely in the driver's seat with a firm grasp on the steering wheel. From social media to online publications and databases, however, today's leaders have little say over who has access to details about their lives. In many ways, they are passengers in a car with limited control over where they're headed.

Today's restaurants and hair salons cannot stop Yelp or Google from publishing profiles about their businesses that anyone can see and contribute to. Similarly, leaders are being made transparent and held to a degree of accountability without their consent. During these times of the unprecedented spread of information and misinformation about people and organizations, Leaders carry a heavy burden. Managing transparency and accountability is a matter of their professional survival. Doing both well requires Leaders to identify and then skillfully navigate what they can control or manage.

In all phases of your career—whether you have been in positional leadership for years, are assuming new responsibilities within your present one, or have joined a new organization—you're responsible for clearly articulating your organization's purpose and establishing expectations.

Practices must be put in place in order for organizations to execute their purpose. Leaders have their hand on the pulse of all parts of their operations. They reward positive outcomes and accomplishments. Leaders don't play favorites; support is equitable and fair and based on what is necessary to reach a particular goal.

Whether your organization is big or small, making your purpose clear to everyone and developing an effective means of receiving regular feedback is key to ensuring your organization's purpose is being fulfilled. Feedback takes various forms, both direct and indirect.

Direct feedback is explicit. Examples include a CEO making a presentation in front of a leadership team during an official meeting where an open discussion ensues and directives are drafted after; written replies respondents provide in surveys leaders have solicited; summary notes of a meeting; reports leaders have designated others give them; and verbal responses people provide leaders during one-on-one gatherings in a formal setting or through informal conversation.

In general, direct feedback involves describing a specific problem. Frequently, a leader then solicits input on how to solve it. This may be sought during a structured discussion about an organization's objectives that has used data to measure everyone's work and progress. For example, in a meeting with stakeholders, a CEO may say, "Here's the problem. Sales are down 20 percent this quarter. What do we do to increase our numbers?"

Indirect feedback is nonverbal, subtle, nuanced, and equally as important as its direct counterpart. From sayings such as "It's important to read between the lines" to Peter Drucker's aphorism, "The most important thing in communication is to hear what isn't being said,"[1] our culture understands that indirect feedback is a basic form of communication. The moment we begin expressing ourselves to our primary caregivers, we've learned to both read and give indirect feedback.

You often receive indirect and direct feedback at the same time. You may be having a one-on-one conversation and ask a question. You'll receive direct feedback by way of the person's verbal reply. Concurrently, the indirect feedback may be a smile or tensing of the forehead. Or it may be a relaxed posture or a rigid one. The words the person expresses may or may not align with his or her body language. And observing this form of indirect feedback provides you as a Leader with important information that requires attention.

We see the essential role of indirect feedback in today's device-driven communications. Or more specifically, we see the consequences of the lack of it. Imagine picking up your smartphone and becoming upset after reading an email, text, tweet, or direct message from your friend. Its content provides little to no indirect feedback. Facial expressions, intonation, and posture do not accompany these words. But on their own, what appears on our screen rankles our nerves.

Now imagine those exact words expressed in a one-on-one conversation where we also receive indirect feedback. The very same message that offended us on our mobile device could elicit the opposite response when taking place during an in-person interaction. Rather than annoyed or offended, we find the smile and the comical way the person delivers his message amusing, and they make us laugh. The indirect feedback this person provided in this example is just as important as the direct feedback it coincided with.

1 Peter Drucker, interview by Bill Moyers, *A World of Ideas,* November 17, 1988, https://billmoyers.com/content/peter-drucker/.

A honed and keen ability to interpret indirect feedback is a powerful problem-solving tool. Accurately understanding indirect feedback is a part of a Leader's ability to address issues early on. From participating in midday water cooler conversations where you ask how something can be improved to observing body language of participants during board meetings, indirect feedback can be the key opening a door that has otherwise been closed to you.

Perhaps productivity has decreased, or goals aren't being met. By tapping into indirect communication, you may finally realize an impasse or obstacle exists that you hadn't recognized before. Maybe people have disagreed with a certain course of action your organization is taking, or they have wanted to express something to you but have been reluctant to do so. It may be only through their indirect feedback that you see there is valuable information you need to hear or an issue that warrants further investigation beyond what others say.

By accurately reading indirect feedback, you'll have the information necessary to decide what course of action you'll take. You may choose to find out more, take drastic action, or do nothing—whichever the case, awareness rather than ignorance has guided your decision.

A Leader's combined direct and indirect feedback comprises:

- identifying a specific problem and articulating it;
- seeking feedback, which includes considering options through listening to others' perspectives;
- creating a summary that highlights areas of disagreement and consensus;
- possibly arranging another meeting where stakeholders review the summary and express additional opinions and concerns;
- creating an action plan that outlines the path, strategies, series of activities, people responsible (including the lead person), timelines, benchmarks, budget needed to execute the plan, and deadlines;

- executing the action plan;
- gaining any knowledge through its implementation;
- modifying the action plan as necessary;
- measuring and reviewing the outcomes of the action plan to see the extent to which the problem was solved.

When Leaders effectively implement opportunities for feedback, they encourage others to contribute and thus be invested in reaching the milestones necessary to achieve major goals. In each step, clear and definite communication is key. When it comes to problem-solving, there is no room for ambiguity. Throughout this process, a champion is usually designated. This is because solving big problems is arduous—the more individuals, departments, and divisions involved, the greater the likelihood of bottlenecks.

As with any complex and difficult undertaking, becoming distracted and losing momentum are expected. While all stakeholders are part of problem-solving, a champion will both oversee and hold all participants responsible and accountable. He or she prevents the organization from veering off course and slowing down and coordinates individuals, groups, and processes. And more importantly, the champion is ultimately held responsible for the outcome.

For Emerging Leaders, There's No Such Thing as Casual Conversation

Supervisors regularly ask emerging Leaders for their direct feedback—often in a one-on-one setting. The value of these Leaders' viewpoints increases when they choose their words carefully and uphold high professional standards in expressing themselves. In other words, although the setting may be casual, emerging Leaders benefit from communicating in the same way they would during a high-stakes formal meeting.

An informal setting with your boss may mislead you into thinking you can say whatever you want. Leaders may be having a meal at a restaurant with their supervisor, attending a conference or social event with him or her, bump into their boss in an elevator or hallway, or have an unplanned one-on-one conversation before or after a meeting. They may interpret conversations with a boss under these informal contexts as casual. The setting may be similar to one where a Leader has met with friends or family countless times before. But make no mistake; while the surroundings may be informal, it's important to err on the side of caution.

Casual settings can be deceptive. A bustling bar, a fun social event, a relaxing meal after an intense conference day . . . you may feel free to unwind in the company of your supervisor, who may seem more like your friend than your boss now. But even when you may be motivated to do otherwise, maintain professional decorum whenever you're communicating with your supervisor. When in doubt, playing it safe means staying within the boundaries of your work role.

The risk of a casual setting is it can result in behavior that others interpret as inappropriate, unprofessional, or lacking in reasonable, clear thinking. To avoid this, maintain the direct and indirect communication skills you've honed throughout your career. Even if the CEO is behaving casually, emerging Leaders most often benefit from upholding their workplace standards, no matter what the setting.

Whether informal or formal, when emerging Leaders can express their perspective to their supervisors, this may present a moment for them to shine. Thus they need to take these opportunities with the utmost care. At the same time, while you may see an opening to introduce your point, your supervisor may still dismiss your idea. Even your most articulately expressed and logical explanations, in the end, may not be part of a supervisor's final decision. This could be because he or she disagrees with what you propose or the timing of bringing up your point may not be right for innumerable reasons—the simplest of which is your boss may not be in a listening mood.

If your supervisor decides not to act in accordance with what you suggested, you may be compelled to continue expressing your opinion. You may be concerned about the consequences that will arise from not taking a particular course of action. In many cases, however, when emerging

Leaders continue to push their agendas, they may jeopardize their professional position. This risk may be worthwhile if the issue is critical enough, but by continuing to pursue it, their efforts may backfire. Unfortunately, no clear formula exists to know when to continue pushing and when to back off.

For emerging Leaders, honing their judgment is essential to achieving their objectives. They use their discernment to determine when they should tenaciously pursue an agenda (which may require bold action in order to experience a payoff) versus when they should kill an idea, no matter how good it is. Also, context matters. Catch a boss on a bad day, and an idea you propose that would otherwise result in interest could be dead on arrival.

To add further complexity, the identical setting could result in failure or success. On the one hand, in loud, crowded bars, the noise and distraction are far from conducive to having a thoughtful one-on-one conversation. On the other hand, brilliant ideas have been hatched from impromptu notes frantically scribbled on tiny cocktail napkins by two people standing practically elbow to elbow drinking beers. There is no clear path to figure out when to boldly move forward and when to ease off.

Sometimes people decide to circumvent direct communication with their supervisor by expressing their opinions to colleagues, either verbally or through emails. They may be motivated to keep information from a supervisor in order to create support for their proposal, that is, lobbying for their idea before presenting it. Or they may be keeping it from a supervisor for a wholly self-serving purpose. Both are usually rookie moves that will most likely backfire.

At the same time, there are times when sharing ideas with colleagues is a prudent practice that helps a person vet and formulate his or her ideas. When doing so is a means to present a well-developed concept to a supervisor rather than a way to keep an idea from him or her, this is the opposite of a subversive act. It is an instance of sharing ideas, collaborating, brainstorming with colleagues, and harnessing collective creative energy. The main purpose is to present the most compelling case possible to a supervisor.

Keep in mind that most supervisors have a strict "no surprise policy." This means they want to be informed as important ideas unfold and evolve within their departments or organizations. The intent is not to micromanage but, rather, to maintain trust and to avoid being alarmed with new information and perceived as unaware of the work employees are performing.

For example, during a board meeting, a supervisor is told about something she had no prior knowledge about. Now she's tasked to provide her opinion. She doesn't have the data and time necessary to make an intelligent observation. It's as if she has been struck by a rogue wave. She feels embarrassed and, at worst, ambushed. This casts a negative light on the person who broached the subject with his or her boss.

Trusting one's wisdom, combined with trial-and-error practice, is how Leaders increase the likelihood of getting people on their side and having what they believe in considered by others.

In addition, every workplace culture is different. Compared to today's positional Leaders, previous ones held much more unquestioned authority. Contemporary Leaders emphasize collaboration and participation. The longer Leaders are in positional leadership roles with a consistent team, the more likely they work efficiently and effectively together.

With that said, in order to evolve, Leaders benefit by continually introducing new people into the organization who provide effective and innovative perspectives. By emphasizing inclusion and teamwork, Leaders avoid problems that arise in more authoritarian organizations.

Today's positional Leaders create a culture where people's opinions are valued. That doesn't mean each perspective will be the basis of a particular decision. But during the phase of seeking feedback, participants are encouraged to provide their input. Positional Leaders steer away from the black-and-white label of opinions being right or wrong or of someone winning or losing.

Rather, all perspectives contribute to the final path chosen. For instance, within a leadership team meeting, participants are given the chance to pitch in. They are allowed to raise their concerns and express what they think are downsides to a particular course of action, which influence their recommendation.

Whether you're dealing with a company with a strict authoritarian leadership or a broad, shared, decision-making model, at some point a person in charge must finalize or approve a particular direction. This may have been determined by one person (although today's leaders rarely take unilateral action) or through active consensus (which is the more common strategy). Once this direction has been agreed upon, the expectation is that all participants will follow the action plan, create a positive outcome, and share in its failures and successes. Even with consensus, however, one person is ultimately in charge.

Many aspiring and emerging leaders dream of being the person spearheading an action plan. This is the moment they've been preparing for their entire careers. It signals a new stage of growth and opportunity. But often, aspiring leaders aren't prepared for the huge amount of pressure associated with their newfound responsibility. While many crumble under such strain, Leaders are able to overcome it and by doing so gain immense satisfaction from taking on more and greater responsibility.

Through the full feedback process, the person in charge of the action plan has provided ample opportunities for everyone to express an opinion. While modification and course correction are to be expected in the days, weeks, and months ahead, second-guessing of the direction itself is often counterproductive and can be downright disruptive.

Doing so may label you as a naysayer and complainer who sees obstacles instead of opportunities. Rather than helpful, you may be viewed as an aggravating annoyance who slows down the organization, including its problem-solving process.

At the same time, when participants identify problems that require a superior's attention, they are responsible to bring these up to that individual. This is not the same as naysaying or complaining, because it focuses on improving the action plan rather than questioning it.

Keeping superiors abreast of major issues that may result in failure is a participant's duty. Upper-level leaders are ultimately responsible for the outcome, but because participants are closely tied to the project at the implementation level, they may have direct insight that their bosses do not. For participants to have these conversations is difficult, but doing so is essential. Facilitating and encouraging such dialogue are part of a strong evaluation process.

Among the many benefits of a well-designed process is that it provides opportunities for participants to bring up problems that may require course correction. ADLI (approach, deployment, learning, integration) is one example of a well-respected strategy, developed by the Baldrige Performance Excellence Program.[2] The evaluation is based on the following:

- **Approach:** The methods your organization uses to carry out its processes
- **Deployment:** The extent to which your organization applies an approach in relevant work units throughout your organization
- **Learning:** New knowledge or skills acquired through evaluation, study, experience, and innovation
- **Integration:** The harmonization of plans, processes, information, resource decisions, workforce capability and capacity, actions, results, and analyses to support key organization-wide goals

A sound process such as ADLI keeps teams accountable and focused and allows for consensus building. At each stage, participants provide input, including highlighting issues and recommending modifications to keep a project on track.

2 Harry Hertz, "The Baldrige Criteria Are Insufficient," Baldrige: The Official Baldrige Blog, October 25, 2018, https://www.nist.gov/blogs/blogrige/baldrige-criteria-are-insufficient.

The Importance of Workplace Protocols

These are systems designed to engender harmony within an organization by means of high productivity, effectiveness, and goal achievement. Workflow protocols provide a common framework that everyone commits to regarding performing and accomplishing a specific task. These reinforce the interdependence among an organization's segments, such as between its divisions and departments.

An organization's ability to meet its most ambitious goals is contingent on individuals working together to meet common, clearly articulated objectives. When a Leader's vision aligns with practical implementation, such as workflow protocols, then the organization moves in a positive direction.

Workflow protocols make the goals of the organization relevant to its employees. By understanding this interdependence, employees see the part they play within the broader organization. Workflow protocols also facilitate a Leader's ability to hold divisions, departments, and individuals accountable. When everyone in an organization knows his or her role, Leaders are able to measure individual and group progress.

Employees move in and out of divisions and departments. With workflow protocols in place, new employees have the information necessary to quickly learn the structure that guides their department and greater organization. This increases efficiency by reducing the likelihood of bottlenecks and obstacles that happen when individuals aren't clear on their roles and responsibilities.

Without a workflow protocol, dissonance arises. Communication breaks down within and between divisions and departments. Inevitably, poor outcomes occur, and goals aren't met. Without a clear means of being able to hold particular people accountable, individuals blame others for dismal performance. These workplace conditions add further adversity to already difficult circumstances when an organization hits an obstacle.

Workflow protocols decrease the likelihood of missteps and errors that keep an organization from progressing toward its goals. Inevitably, however, no matter how effective an organization implements workflow protocols, human error will take place.

People make mistakes, and Leaders understand this. Leaders give their team members the space and tools to correct reasonable and logical errors. Leaders benefit by creating a workplace where people are encouraged to admit when they've made mistakes, analyze what happened, correct them as soon as possible, and make adjustments and modifications so they will not repeat them. This plays a role in an organization's commitment to continuous improvement.

Mistakes are understood as opportunities for an organization and its members to grow, learn, and improve. When Leaders model a spirit of improvement, they set their organizations up to productively address changes both internally and externally.

When Leaders are appointed to oversee an action plan and held responsible for its outcome, they benefit from debriefs. These are formal or informal meetings that serve as status checks. They may be scheduled immediately if an urgent matter requires prompt attention. Frequent debriefs review the main points of an activity within an action plan. The better organized the debrief, the more effective it is. Its goal is to increase the likelihood that participants succeed. Executive coaches often use these with their clients. Frequent debriefs do the following:

- Evaluate progress
- Clarify the significant points or aspects of the plan
- Solve problems
- Avoid problems before they happen
- Quickly identify and discard wasteful activity
- Establish timelines or sequences of actions
- Help the Leader maintain momentum as he or she works through the action plan

- Keep participants focused on and gain mastery of the specific tasks they are charged to accomplish
- Increase the likelihood that participants succeed in what they are tasked to do

Summary

What you've learned so far provides the foundational practices Leaders need to skillfully move forward with their ambitious objectives. While these strategies are a must for good managers, Leaders require the added step of getting people on their side.

On the most basic level, your team or organization members must meet the day-to-day requirements of their jobs to a satisfactory degree—an effective manager will see that they do this. Beyond that, your team or organization members must be motivated, focused, and fully committed to embracing the challenges and triumphs of what they're responsible to accomplish. This is where Leaders stand out from leaders.

Organizations that excel in quality and performance are those where positional Leaders have mastered the art of getting employees on their side. Mediocre companies plagued by a status quo–oriented culture have experienced dramatic turnarounds by Leaders who have done this well. As a result, their organizations have reached superior achievement and outcomes besting competitors. In the next chapter, you'll learn how they do this: by establishing the initial relationship between Leader and follower.

Chapter 5

GETTING PEOPLE ON YOUR SIDE, PART 2

Education is the ability to listen to almost anything without losing your temper or your self-confidence.

—ROBERT FROST

LEADERS WHO HAVE moved into C-level positions have done so by following one of two paths. They either rose through their organization's ranks or were brought in from the outside. Whether coming from the inside or outside, they bring with them a history, background, and reputation. The saying "your current job is your interview for your next job" reflects this. The characteristics you are known for can be viewed as baggage or gifts.

If you are promoted within your organization and you've spent a considerable amount of time as a middle-level leader, those around you know your communication style, your beliefs, how you deal with stress, and how sincere and trustworthy you are. Career advancement under these circumstances is viewed as either a welcome addition to the highest leadership level or a dreadful and long-term inconvenience. This point is important because the loyalty and commitment from your subordinates had been established long before you were appointed to your new position.

If a leader's reputation is negative, turning it positive may take a long time, requiring persistent new behavior to undo the damage. But if it's positive, the path to future success has been made much easier by a leader who is perceived as honest, compassionate, fair, and strong.

If you are promoted from outside, your reputation still precedes you. Word travels fast, particularly within smaller industries, and those around you know about you long before you show up for your first day on the job. In the past, information about you may have been leaked through your screening and interview process.

Today, X (formerly Twitter), Instagram, LinkedIn, Facebook, and more make it impossible for Leaders to avoid public scrutiny. People use information from social media to draw their conclusions about you before they meet you face-to-face. So how do you establish an initial relationship with your team when so much information precedes you?

While much of what others perceive of you is out of your control, you can certainly take charge of your actions toward others. Dressing well, having a confident posture, and presenting a cordial, calm, pleasant, engaging, and friendly demeanor leave an impression that builds confidence and credibility.

A standoffish, overly formal, arrogant, insecure, and distant attitude accompanied by fidgety nervousness leaves a first impression that disappoints and does not engender confidence. Nor is it likely to lead to a promising future. The positive reputation that precedes you by word of mouth and your online presence can be erased if you come across as disingenuous. A professional demeanor you've mastered to the point where you express it naturally shows others who you are and what you stand for.

People at the highest levels are always improving themselves. They may attend Toastmasters to hone their public speaking and belong to executive groups such as Vistage International and YPO (Young Presidents' Organization). Activities such as these provide growth and improve their leadership. Leaders groom themselves to be in the public eye from the start of their careers.

For today's emerging Leaders, draw a plan for yourself early on. This includes a leadership style you are comfortable with that is compatible with your sector and the future vision you hold for yourself. By considering how you will behave and act as your career unfolds, you'll find yourself performing to that standard. Allocating time for preparing yourself to assume your role in positional leadership will benefit you as you grow and gain expertise in your chosen field.

Verbal Communication

Leaders are under a perpetual microscope. The nature of their position of power means people pay attention to what they say and how they say it. Those closest to a Leader become skilled at interpreting his or her words.

Whether you're speaking in a formal or informal setting, polite, clear, and concise communication is crucial. While there's room for personal and lighthearted conversation, at the center of all your communication are business and a specific task at hand.

The way you speak leaves a lasting impression, so choose your words and how you express them carefully. People expect Leaders to have mastery over the spoken word and to consistently speak at a highly professional level. In today's fast-paced, social media–heavy world, carefully considered words seem part of a pre-internet age. But Leaders are held to a higher standard than the masses, whose words aren't scrutinized by a captive audience. Thus, laziness or consistent casualness with communication is not an option.

Throughout history, there have been leaders who have taken the opposite tack. Rather than being iron fists in velvet gloves, they've been bulls in china shops. These leaders often don't care, or perhaps even relish in, unrestrained and provocative communication. Their attitude is they are being honest and don't assume responsibility if the listener is offended by what is said. Sometimes those who embrace this style of communication believe that when a person is offended, that's his or her problem and, in fact, reflects personal weakness on the listener's part.

In most cases, Leaders should avoid taking on this minority perspective. While it may have served a leader well or a leader may have succeeded *despite* this communication approach, I can point to many instances where such a speaking style stifled professional advancement or even crushed a person's career. In other words, embracing offensive communication is not the formula for success. Rather, in most cases, it harms a person's career. In addition, it attracts hostile conflict. This is the opposite of getting people on your side and runs the risk of leading to burnout and stress-related illness, such as depression, anxiety, and hypertension—all enemies of long-term success.

The power that comes with leadership means Leaders have an ethical obligation to speak in a manner that respects others, upholds the highest values of their profession, and unifies rather than divides people. Leaders have the duty to cultivate and model appropriate speech for themselves and within their organizations. This means upholding civility and respect and never demeaning others.

At the same time, in today's public square, you'll be hard pressed to find a topic that won't offend. Despite a Leader's best intentions to maintain cultured and civil discourse, he or she will inevitably rankle someone's nerves.

Journalists and social media players can easily twist even the most innocuous words, remove them from context, and suddenly generate widespread outrage. This is the world we live and work in and is one of the pressures today's Leaders face. Staying true to your values and expressing them often means what you say will attract criticism and even downright opposition—particularly if that view is outside the majority. But regardless of how controversial or against the current your perspective is, you can hold and then express your position while maintaining dignity and civility. This practice is essential to getting people on your side.

To uphold civil discourse, find a speaking pace that is comfortable for you. Express yourself sincerely, honestly, and compassionately. Be clear and definite—wishy-washy and noncommittal are the opposite of sincere. Choose your message wisely, which requires you to use language relevant to your audience. Model the values you want to see in others. Your leadership style, vision, and purpose as they relate to your organization express themselves through your word choice, syntax, eye contact, and tone of voice.

In the event you are hired to perform a major turnaround, you want to put people at ease. Yes, the work ahead will be difficult, but avoid describing the complete challenges the department, division, or organization faces all at once. You are already in the difficult place of having to make decisions that will inevitably be subject to criticism, so selecting your words carefully will make your job easier going forward.

When speaking before an audience—small or large—avoid reading from a script. You'll see many high-level leaders refer to or read directly from notes. This is not desirable. What you say doesn't always have to be the most articulate. More important is to speak from the heart.

Using talking points or an outline you've memorized ahead of time is far better than reading from a piece of paper. You are perceived as more sincere when you speak without constantly referencing remarks you've prepared. Speaking well without relying on notes is a difficult feat, but investing time practicing and developing amazing public speaking skills will benefit you throughout your career.

While unscripted or minimally scripted is preferred, an impeccably organized message is essential. Expressing your thoughts requires careful consideration on your part. When addressing a problem, begin with background. Explain what happened and what needs to be done. Then communicate the plan, the expectation, and what the outcome should be. Describe how you envision measuring success. Keep your main points to no more than four. More than that, and your audience will likely forget the most important parts of your message. And repeat your points. Three times is a generally accepted number. Using examples and stories generates interest and makes your content relatable. But keep them short, simple, and spread out during your talk. Make sure their role is to emphasize and illustrate your points. Otherwise, they run the risk of moving you away from your main purpose.

Thorough preparation is one way to address the inevitable jitters that arise before giving a talk. Nervousness is normal and often a sign that you're taking your responsibility seriously. When anxiety arises, remind yourself and feel confident that you've prepared as much as possible to deliver your message well.

Be attentive to the words you use. Expanding your vocabulary and selecting words that precisely express an activity demonstrate that you take communication seriously. This does not mean you intentionally pick words that few will understand—that is elitist and will result in others tuning out your message or simply not understanding what you want to convey. For example, the verb *walk* is broad. Words that are more precise and widely understood are *strut, stroll, race, march,* and *rush*. None is pretentious, and each one expresses a meaning beyond simply walking. Your objective when communicating is to speak for understanding and clarity.

Humor, when done well, lightens serious conversation. If you're good at it, then use it sparingly. If you're not good at it, then avoid practicing on your workforce. And never use humor to make fun of anyone—and specifically do not single individuals out in your organization. Today's humor commonly uses profanity—it's accepted in mainstream culture. But part of a Leader's responsibility is to be careful about what he or she says, and that includes being cautious about expletives or vulgar language. Leaders represent the best of their organization, so their words reflect the company's values and mission.

How Do You Present Yourself?

Recent history's greatest Leaders—Martin Luther King Jr., Mother Teresa, Winston Churchill, John F. Kennedy, Pope John Paul II—all had extraordinary charisma and a commanding presence. Watching today's Leaders demonstrate their skill is remarkable to witness. Through their magnetism and enthusiasm, they inspire devotion, loyalty, and passion in others. That they have been able to influence and operate in the public eye for so long demonstrates the mark they've left on society. Their leadership is powerful and transcends distance and time. Often Leaders are so persuasive that they can convince others to go to great lengths to realize the cause for which they advocate. Long after history's famous Leaders have passed away, their philosophy, doctrine, message, or cause continues to inspire and fascinate people.

Many Leaders are affable, approachable, and focused. Sometimes the power of their presence alone is enough to compel others to act. While Leaders may have their opinions, they do not force others to agree. Rather, they are clear and honest in delivering the content of their message. This is the sign of confidence and strength. Leaders present what they believe is true to influence others.

In our daily lives, these people are our teachers, lawyers, clergy, politicians, and community advocates. They are those we see at our jobs. Leaders have a vision and devote their lives to the work that brings about the change they believe is necessary and possible. When it comes to our own leadership path, we convince and motivate others to join our cause in two ways.

First, we know who we are. This includes our strengths, weaknesses, and commitment to remaining faithful to our values. Part of this self-awareness comes from introspection and reflection. We are pledged to continually evolving because we realize that growth will motivate us to learn, adapt to change, and increase our capacity for compassion and empathy. We do not look for a finish line to cross when it comes to our professional development. Instead, we reach one goal and then set another. Leadership extends beyond the workplace and is part of our innate character, which informs all aspects of our lives.

Second, we have a clear understanding of our purpose. An organization's strategic plan reflects the degree to which a Leader understands the purpose and function of the organization, as well as his or her role in it. A

Leader's ability to steer the organization and its stakeholders toward high achievement relies on knowledge of how the organization is currently operating and how it will move forward to a new and better place.

Seeing how the moving parts of the organization work toward a common objective is not easy. The bigger the business, the more it is multifaceted, which increases ambiguity and conflicting approaches to achieve desired outcomes. Nevertheless, the organization's Leader typically has the best understanding of its current status. Meanwhile, others will have their own ideas and perspectives. Their insights and input can improve plans and activities the positional Leader is responsible to oversee.

Leaders uphold transparency. This includes demonstrating the level of commitment they have and the work ethic they maintain to do their jobs. They are always improving themselves and model this commitment to continual refinement to their team members. In addition, they expect others to improve themselves and expand their capabilities as well. That is to say, the same high expectations Leaders place on themselves, they place on others.

One of the marks of a Leader is the ability to mentor others in the organization to succeed. Leaders nurture and train their team members to achieve the highest levels of expertise for themselves. Thus a Leader is a facilitator and teacher.

An organization is only as good as the people within it and the resources they use to meet objectives. Data, for example, allow companies to measure progress, correct or moderate activity, and hold individuals accountable. It takes a strong and talented team of men and women to properly interpret and use this information. Effective Leaders are skilled at hiring and training people who will move their organization forward. They are knowledgeable, are supportive, and understand how the divisions, departments, and individuals that work within them operate.

Knowing our purpose and who we are is reflected in how we present ourselves as Leaders to those within our organizations. We also seek to surround ourselves with people who believe in our vision and are willing to put forth their best effort in accomplishing desired outcomes.

The Importance of Emotional Intelligence

Success in any endeavor requires self-awareness. An understanding of who you are and how you manage yourself will guide your actions. Through reflection, failure, and success, we learn what we are made of. For many Leaders, mastery over their emotions is more important than their physical abilities. Uncontrolled emotions are typically associated with erratic behavior, and the result is ineffective leadership. Leaders who habitually display emotional outrage are rarely successful in bringing teams to a place where they are at ease in sharing or collaborating with others.

Stress and conflict are mental states that affect our physical well-being. As we deepen our self-awareness, we know what comes easy to us and what doesn't. Through practice and repetition, we can overcome areas of weakness. By deepening our self-awareness, we improve our understanding and empathy toward others. We also increase our ability to manage our emotions through self-discipline and self-control. Rather than turn to alcohol, drugs, or other addictions to deal with stress, we implement strategies to enhance our well-being.

We will inevitably be confronted with men and women who don't manage their emotions well. They have a psychological immaturity that can manifest in hateful, aggressive, and volatile behavior. Their negativity can cause stress, anger, mistrust, and bitterness in the workplace. In order to skillfully address the negative influences that threaten the positive culture Leaders strive to engender, effective Leaders use their psychological maturity to drive their decisions.

Leaders that exhibit emotional stability model the same behavior in others. But because the way in which people interpret another person's emotions is subjective, a calm and even demeanor could be seen as weak, ineffective, and distant. Leaders must be aware of how others may view them and strike a balance between that and the steadiness they wish to convey. If leaders are interpreted as lacking emotion, they may be labeled as uncaring, aloof, and cold. Too much emotion, and leaders may be called threatening and unstable. As long as Leaders are consistently measured and reasonable in their behavior, their benevolence and caring will more likely be interpreted as a strength rather than a weakness.

Leaders celebrate and honor their workforce, rather than treat them like mere producers on a positive or negative balance sheet. When individuals within an organization underperform, this rarely signifies incompetence. A Leader uses discernment to identify areas of weakness in others and provides guidance on how they can improve, including where they can obtain information and support. The success of all employees rests in the Leader's ability to clearly establish and convey what is expected of them. At a minimum, a Leader directs employees toward the resources they need to accomplish their tasks.

Body Language and Dress

Arms folded, a tense forehead, and eyes cast down versus outstretched arms, a smile, and eye contact . . . each conveys entirely different messages requiring no words. The gestures and movements we make are sometimes conscious but most of the time unconscious. Nonverbal communication often speaks louder than words and frequently plays a significant role in how effectively Leaders convey what they seek to express.

In the appropriate situation, Leaders benefit by using the cues we commonly associate with being open, positive, and engaging, as well as in other circumstances with being closed, negative, and aloof. They can consciously use their body language to express positive and negative emotions with others.

Leaders can also use body language to assert their strength and health. This often requires self-awareness. If your tendency is to slouch, this will affect how your audience interprets your words. You may be delivering an uplifting and positive message, but if your posture doesn't show this, your words may not be accepted as you intended.

While you may see changing your body language as being superficial and insincere, the alternative—changing societal conditioning—is not going to happen. Our facial expression and posture reflect our attitude and what we're thinking. Leaders benefit by learning to align their non-verbal communication with their verbal statements. More importantly, they gain immensely from the self-control and discipline required to express composure and calm, regardless of their current emotional state. Doing so helps us reach the outcomes we desire when communicating with others.

Next, every professional organization, either implicitly or explicitly, has dress standards. Whatever the rules, always be conscious of what's acceptable and stay within those guidelines. Your career is in constant change because you've committed to growth. But during these shifts remember perception is everything.

When making your clothing decisions, keep in mind the type of work you perform and your administrative level. Consider being the best-dressed person in the room. This tells those around you that you want to be taken seriously, you respect and strive to uphold workplace dress standards, and you seek to make a positive impression.

Your appearance, body language, and speaking style heavily influence how your ideas and contributions will be received. If your goal is to have your perspective considered and adopted, then the simple act of taking your appearance seriously is an effective first step to meeting your objective. What I'm proposing here isn't intended to put you into debt upgrading your wardrobe. That would be irresponsible advice. Rather, I recommend investing time and energy into planning your appearance and making wise purchasing decisions if necessary.

Casual business attire is more and more acceptable within the workplace. Meanwhile, the home has become a more formal place as a result of more people working full-time from their houses. In either setting, business attire largely relies on context. What you wear to work daily may not be the same as your clothing choices during important meetings and gatherings. In order to follow the rules to a high degree, observe, learn, and speak to experienced colleagues that you respect. While at times you may decide to veer from the expected path, make sure you properly assess the pluses and minuses of doing so.

Getting People on Your Side Is More Important than Winning

Throughout the day, leaders meet and speak with many people. Each conversation is important. Some conversations may seem insignificant because they don't directly move a project forward. But consider that each one contributes to and reinforces the communication culture between team members and positional leaders.

When you're introducing an idea, checking on the status of implementation, or improving the process to operationalize and integrate work, Leaders benefit by understanding the importance of managing conversations connected to these topics.

Whether within groups or one-on-one, the Leader is responsible to steer conversations back toward their primary purpose when they veer off course. Doing so isn't always easy and often requires well-honed skills. When one of the expected outcomes of a discussion is to pick the best option among many, you may see the benefit of using the process of elimination. The formula of making a point followed by encouraging and listening to counterpoints is often an effective version of the process-of-elimination strategy.

Leaders are tasked to prioritize the importance of topics of discussion, resolve points of disagreement, and move a conversation forward. Sometimes Leaders benefit by starting with topics that all participants can agree on (non-contentious points are usually less important ones). By doing so, Leaders may gain support from the larger group, as long as participants are clear about the broader goal and what the Leader seeks to accomplish.

Choosing one's battles well is a skill all Leaders have. When a discussion turns aggressively negative, the Leader is charged to evaluate whether to continue fighting or declare a truce and move on. Asking yourself what impact the contentious topic will have on creating and building teamwork is one way to assess the amount of attention you'll allocate toward continuing the discussion.

If selecting and affirming a team committed to accomplishing a need within your organization is hampered by a clash of differing ideas, then the best option may be to move on rather than continue the battle. Leaders realize winning a verbal exchange is only a short-term gain if it impedes coming to agreement on bigger and more important topics.

Some participants provide contrarian opinions to insert themselves into a discussion and assert their relevance to the group. In these instances, they're not driven by the conviction of driving home a point they believe is important. By identifying this behavior, Leaders know dwelling on a subject being pressed by such individuals is a waste of time.

Ultimately having your agenda move forward to reach the outcome you seek sometimes requires conceding defeat on smaller battles. You may disagree with the person who's opposing your view and realize you're right, but Leaders have an acute understanding of the long term. Knowing the big picture means, when you see fit, you allow such contentious people to have their point acknowledged and accepted rather than denied. As long as they are speaking their truth in a reasonable and professional manner, their perspective may be worth acknowledging as valuable. They must, however, be willing to accept the overarching outcome. A team member's consistent pattern of obstructing, rejecting, and undermining requires your attention.

On the one hand, this behavior may signal professional immaturity. With mentoring and other professional development support, this person may eventually grow and align with your organization's culture. One possible outcome of conciliatory gestures on your part with team members who disagree with you is a deepening of mutual trust. The respect you gain with this person can lead to immense benefit in the long run. Weeks, months, or even years later, he or she may provide the support that will take you far into the future.

On the other hand, inappropriate or bad behavior may signal that this person is not a good fit on your team. Without letting him or her go, this person will consume your organization's time and effort and create disharmony. The potential for someone to inject poison into a company's culture must be addressed right away. Otherwise, the damage caused may take years to undo and can even lead to a company's demise. Fortunately, a person infusing that level of toxicity is rare.

Regardless of the degree of difficulty within a meeting, always attempt to end each discussion with a review for clarity, an offer of support, or an insight that guides the next steps forward. Doing so is one example of how Leaders maintain objectivity, which in this instance means acting in their organization's best interest, even when tensions run high. Staying calm under pressure earns the respect of their team.

Be a Patient Listener

A Leader's daily agenda is full. But no matter how packed their calendars, Leaders are charged to provide their teams with reassurance and support. They don't have the luxury to use being busy as an excuse to stop doing the tasks ascribed to them. Often a team seeks its Leader's support beyond the work setting.

While most Leaders aren't licensed clinical psychologists, the respect for their accomplishments and their perceived wisdom compels others to seek their advice. People see Leaders as successful and capable men and women who may hold answers and provide guidance. Others may come seeking affirmation and acceptance. Leaders should never assume the role of a mental health professional, but they certainly can be a source of support. In this role, Leaders are master listeners. They understand that effective listening is one of their responsibilities. And they consistently provide their full attention to others.

To listen well, maintain thoughtful eye contact. Too little and you'll be perceived as aloof or distracted. Too much and you'll make the listener uncomfortable. Other nonverbal expressions that show you're listening are head nodding, empathetic expressions (smiling or tensing your forehead), and open hands and arms.

If you've begun an impromptu conversation or one that requires more time than you've allocated, schedule a period when you can both continue the discussion. Because your time is limited, you must be selective with whom and for how long you'll meet. When you determine getting together is appropriate, fully commit. This means scheduling enough time so the conversation isn't filled with interruptions. In general, one-on-one meetings build loyalty and trust.

In group settings, one strategy to listening well is to assume others don't have the background information you have. In fact, often Leaders are privy to information they're not allowed to share. Although in some instances, every individual you're meeting has worked with you for years and understands you and your expectations, this is rare. In most instances, the tactic of assuming that no one in the group knows what you do will steer you toward actions that demonstrate higher-quality listening.

Provide information by gradually sharing content that encourages questions and input from others. When you listen to inquiries and comments, act as if you don't have background information about those asking you questions. This helps you maintain objectivity and avoid bias that could influence how you interpret what you hear. To illustrate what can happen without seeking more information, here's an often-told story.

One morning, Johnny asked, "Mommy, where did I come from?"

The mother panicked. Her maternal instinct to both protect her six-year-old son's innocence and maintain honesty put her in a thorny parenting dilemma.

She thought he was way too young to hear a lesson about sex. At the same time, she didn't want to deceive him with a myth like the silly stork story. She wondered if she should wait and seek her husband's input first.

"When in doubt, co-parent," she told herself.

In the end, she decided to err on the side of caution and address the question together with her spouse when the three were together in the evening. She told Johnny she'd get back to him later with an answer.

Meanwhile, she searched on her smartphone for expert advice to what she imagined was a common parental predicament. She also texted her best friend about what she should do.

During dinnertime, Mom, Dad, and Johnny sat at the table. Anxious, she broached the subject.

"Johnny asked me today where he came from," she said to her husband.

Immediately, she regretted her words. She was convinced she should have talked the topic over with her husband first and worried she had caught him off-guard. Now he would be stuck, unprepared to provide an age-appropriate reply.

"You're from Chicago," her husband said.

Johnny was happy to have his question answered.

"Really, Daddy? I already asked Mommy, and she didn't know that," he said.

The mother would have saved herself a lot of time and anxiety had she simply asked her son for clarification about his question in the first place. Instead, she assumed she knew what he meant, and this resulted in a series of unnecessarily stressful actions on her part.

In your case, with an open and unprejudiced mind, you'll ask questions for clarity when you're in doubt about a question you've heard. That way, you'll avoid drawing conclusions about what you *think* the listener really wants to know.

Leaders are master communicators. They are charged to deliver messages that influence the entire organization. Thus, they carefully consider the words they use and how their choices will be received and comprehended by their listeners.

Widespread adoption of what you propose may come down to the quality of your pitch. Simply being satisfied with getting your message across is not the mark of a Leader. Instead, Leaders view success as the degree to which they inspire and persuade others to join the cause.

To communicate at this optimal level requires preparation. For others to take your proposal seriously, you first must take your responsibility seriously to deliver your message well. This typically requires days, rather than minutes, of work in advance, so allocate ample time prior to your meeting for refining your delivery.

In order to captivate and energize others, think deeply about your audience. Imagine engaging each participant and not just one group or faction in attendance. If your presentation is focused on a specific aspect of your organization, invite only those who will be invested in the work to be done.

If what you present is not relevant to someone, then consider not having that person participate. Avoid wasting employees' time. This not only deflates them; it also squanders company resources that could otherwise be directed toward productive endeavors. Consider the setting of where you'll present, the timing, the events before and after your meeting, and the prior knowledge your recipients have about the topic of discussion. What you propose may be extremely complicated and require immense background knowledge. No matter how intricate, simplify, simplify, simplify! Reduce your message to succinct talking points.

After you've established your main ideas, now is the time to fine-tune them. This may require changing the order in which you deliver them, revising them, adding or deleting points, and having someone else review them. The order in which you describe key themes and arguments plays an important role in your audience's ability to follow and remember the message.

After you've simplified your message, another oratory tool is to repeat, repeat, repeat! Make your points, define concepts that require common understanding, and then reinforce your message by stating it again. Subtle repetition is key. You want to gracefully reintroduce concepts that remind readers of your most important arguments or concepts, rather than repeat in a way that sounds more like a teacher drilling lessons into her students. People who are hearing a new concept for the first time benefit from repetition that respects their intellect and helps them grasp your main ideas and their deep ramifications. Your audience needs time to consider and reflect while absorbing your message.

When you're introducing new information to an audience, keep in mind that people process and interpret information at different rates. Some draw immediate conclusions about what they heard. Others may need minutes, hours, or even days to thoroughly consider your message and absorb its meaning. Your presentation may describe major changes within the organization or your listeners' division, department, or position within the company. Content of such deep and widespread consequence requires careful consideration on the part of your listeners. They may be downright surprised and seriously affected by what you said to the point where they wonder, "Wow. How did the CEO come up with this? Where did they get this information?" Now they may want to know more, have questions, or offer feedback.

To make your talking points memorable, consider addressing the multiple learning styles of your listeners. By including illustrations, simple graphics, succinct slides, and posters, you will connect directly to your visual learners and connect better with them than by the words you speak.

Two Techniques to Present Information

When it comes to the order in which you present information, you have several options. We'll present two: the anticipatory set and the whole-part-whole approach.

The anticipatory set comes from K through 12 educational lessons. This pedagogical strategy is grounded in research on how we learn and retain new concepts. At the beginning of your presentation, you activate (or connect with) what your audience already knows. One way to do this is through a hook, such as a thought-provoking and memorable story they'll relate to or an anecdote that illustrates where you are headed with your discussion. This short snippet is intended to capture your audience's attention. Sometimes, the element of surprise is effective. That was the intention of the story we presented about Johnny asking his mom where he came from.

After the hook, you deliver your introduction, which may include a brief background and raise a specific problem you're proposing to solve. This forms the bridge between what your group already knows and what you're presenting. Now that you've primed their brains to receive new information, you can go into detail about what you intended your audience to gain from your introduction. You expand upon your introduction and present new vocabulary, define concepts, and propose the actions you want your audience to take, as well as your rationale.

Engage those around you. Once you've earned their attention, you have set up the ideal circumstances to inspire them to reach new professional heights. Your words have the potential to energize them and will provide the spark necessary to develop the mindset for implementing a carefully developed plan.

For example, if you're making a presentation about customer service, after your hook and introduction, you describe what it means to be sensitive to a customer's needs. Part of assessing a customer's needs is to create an environment where he or she feels welcome and comfortable. Now you propose how your organization should do this. Check for understanding by asking questions and pausing for answers, comments, and questions.

You wrap up your presentation by repeating what you covered or discussed. At the end, provide your audience with homework, which may be as simple as a thought-provoking question for them to answer afterward or a formal assignment. In either case, your objective is to make your presentation relevant to your audience by encouraging them to carefully consider what you presented and the role they will play in what you propose.

Next, the whole-part-whole approach begins with asking yourself broad questions in order to organize how you'll present information to your audience. In other words, you take the whole situation and use self-inquiry to break it down into parts. Ask: "What does the current situation look like?" "What changes needed to be made?" "How will changes affect other parts of the process or individual people's work or product?"

By dissecting a problem that needs addressing, you now have the individual components that will drive your discussion. You have the content necessary to refine, rearrange, and organize your presentation in a way that will resonate with your audience and they will understand.

Now that you've developed these parts effectively, you're ready to assemble them into a cohesive talk. From the original whole, you created the two segments you will present to your audience—the individual parts and those parts brought back together into a whole new discussion. When executed effectively, the whole-part-whole results in a delivery that provides a clear picture to your audience of the elements or part of the project that requires their attention and how they can go about improving it. Like a puzzle, you have shown them the individual pieces and how they work together to create the final picture, which is what moves your organization forward. Most importantly, you've described in the clearest and most relevant way possible the role your participants play within the puzzle.

Summary

All the potential leadership skill in the world means nothing if it doesn't produce positive results. Within organizations, high-impact and long-lasting change comes mainly through the teams—not their Leaders. Thus men's and women's reputations as Leaders are measured not by their individual pursuits but rather by what their teams have accomplished and has rippled through the entire organization.

Fundamental to successful teams is getting people on your side. Doing so is accomplished through your verbal and nonverbal communication. Carefully considering the words you say, how you express them, and the questions you ask are key to building credibility with those within your organization. How you present yourself to others, including body language and dress, provide information to those around you that they use to determine the degree to which they trust and respect you.

Getting people on your side consistently throughout your career is fundamental to your long-term success. It comes not by accident but rather through practicing the lessons you've learned in these two chapters. By getting people on your side, you'll build amazing teams, which is how you'll realize your most ambitious vision.

In the next chapter, we'll explore the core qualities that separate managers from Leaders.

Chapter 6

BE AWED BY OTHERS

Nothing is so strong as gentleness,
nothing so gentle as real strength.
—SAINT FRANCIS DE SALES

IN THE INTERNATIONAL bestseller *Blue Ocean Strategy*, the authors, W. Chan Kim and Renée Mauborgne, describe how industries and organizations exist in two oceans: red and blue.[1] The red ocean is stained by competing companies battling among one another, resulting in a blood bath. These are existing businesses and organizations occupying the known market space. The more players enter the ocean, the redder the waters become, each exhibiting its version of *Jaws*—on a mission to gobble up its adversaries. In the red ocean, industries fight over existing and finite wealth. This scarcity further fuels rivalries. When competition increases, all participants have less profit and growth potential.

1 W. Chan Kim and Renée Mauborgne, *Blue Ocean Strategy: How to Create Uncontested Market Space and Make the Competition Irrelevant* (Boston: Harvard Business Review Press, 2015).

Contrast this with the blue ocean. Blue is the color of clear waters, untainted by cutthroat competition. The blue ocean is full of deep and vast opportunity. These are unchartered waters where companies innovate and create new demand. In the blue ocean, organizations are swimming in uncontested market spaces, where they have room to be profitable and grow. Abundant opportunity and immense potential exist. Within the blue ocean, the status quo is challenged, and new paradigms are created that advance industries and even the larger society forward.

Similar to the differences between the red and blue oceans, a wide gulf exists between managers and Leaders. Both managers and Leaders are required to produce excellent results when charged with overseeing a project. While positional Leaders generally possess the prerequisite skills of a manager, the type of projects each is responsible for is one way to differentiate Leaders from managers.

Leaders work on change-oriented projects that move far beyond improving how something is being done. They are responsible to instill new thinking or approaches. Often, a Leader's work has larger implications to an organization than that of managers who are dealing with a company's essential day-to-day operations.

By building a work environment that promotes creativity and the retention of team members committed to facilitating innovation, Leaders make their organizations more effective and competitive. The positional Leader moves an organizational culture to a place that produces a productive and quality-focused workplace.

According to our definition of how managers function, they generally work within a competitive environment, which is the red ocean. Their work often centers on incremental improvements of the product or service with the understanding they need to beat the competition.

Leaders, however, inhabit or strive to swim in the blue ocean. They tackle problem-solving in ways that have resulted in breakthrough products and services. The influence of Leaders within NASA, Netflix, Amazon, and Apple are famous examples. Consider the iTunes Store.

Before Apple released its music retail division, consumers had two choices when it came to buying music. One was brick-and-mortar stores such as Tower Records and the Warehouse, where they could purchase often expensive CDs. The other involved peer-to-peer platforms (such as Napster and LimeWire) where people would upload their music and provide it as a free download to anyone with a computer and internet connection. The entire music industry faced an existential crisis with the peer-to-peer model that was made possible after the online explosion. The industry's revenue-generating model took a massive hit with consumers across the world eagerly participating in a free-for-all download frenzy.

While recording studios and artists scrambled figuring out how to make money in the internet age, the entire music industry seemed doomed. Meanwhile, Apple's foray into playback devices with its highly desirable iPod and its proprietary software, iTunes, gave the company the scale to enter the entrenched music business stuck in its pre-internet revenue model. Initially, iTunes was software with which users organized their music libraries. When Apple opened the iTunes Store in 2003, it launched its online retail space with over two hundred thousand songs available by the world's leading music companies. The company's breakthrough invention, the ninety-nine-cent song, was met with wide skepticism. Why would anyone pay even one penny for a song when non-licensed downloads were free? But as the entertainment industry won court case after court case against peer-to-peer online services, the free services were forced to block their music-downloading features.

Bullish about the iTunes Store's success, when it opened, Steve Jobs said, "Consumers don't want to be treated like criminals and artists don't want their valuable work stolen. The iTunes Music Store offers a groundbreaking solution for both."[2]

A week after its debut, Apple's new product dominated the retail music space with over one million customer downloads.

The music industry sighed a breath of relief knowing it had a viable income-generating model that would protect its artists' most important

2 Apple press release, "Apple Launches the iTunes Music Store," April 28, 2003, https://www.apple.com/newsroom/2003/04/28Apple-Launches-the-iTunes-Music-Store/.

asset—their intellectual property. Apple safely carried them into the internet age. Meanwhile, money poured into Apple's coffers, thanks to its cut from the downloads made from its store.

While brick-and-mortar retailers went to battle against one another vying for ever-shrinking consumer market share, further bloodying their red oceans, Apple embarked on its own journey using its unrivaled music infrastructure. The company sailed free and flourished in the blue ocean and did not spend any time within the red ocean, where its competitors were circling and attacking one another. Apple accelerated the inevitable demise of brick-and-mortar music stores and quickly became one of the world's largest music retailers.

An unstoppable force, Apple expanded by selling TV shows, movies, and an unlimited music subscription service to compete with Spotify and eventually became a content producer.

Apple's iTunes was a major part of its transformation from "Apple Computer" to "Apple," a company that has used its groundbreaking hardware to house its equally cutting-edge software and produce content. The iTunes Store demonstrates one of Apple's many forays into the blue ocean, including mobile devices (the Newton, iPhone, and iPad), entertainment (Apple TV), financial services (Apple Card), healthcare (Apple Watch), and autonomous vehicles.

The remarkable results Leaders produce for their organizations may seem like a process that begins from the top (positional leadership) to the bottom (their teams). But Leaders recognize that amazing ideas spring forth throughout their workforce. Perceptive Leaders are open and always ready to be awed by others. They realize that innovation and substantive change may come from anywhere within their organizations. Nearly every organization has highly inventive individuals within it. They need only know that positional leaders are receptive and always eager to hear new ideas. Leaders who surround themselves with people who feel a freedom to share create workplaces where a blue ocean strategy may flourish.

For such ideas to move from inspiration to implementation and then to positive outcomes, Leaders must maintain an open mind and a sense of humility. Having these qualities is typically associated with deep confidence in oneself. Often people who are insecure about their ability to lead feel threatened by the possibility that someone else has better ideas, talents, or skills. They may interpret the potentially powerful contributions of a subordinate as a possible threat or confirmation of their own weaknesses.

Insecurity is the opposite of the confidence Leaders have in themselves. They realize the mystique surrounding their abilities is, in part, the result of their extraordinary teams. By tapping into the ideas emerging from their individual team members, Leaders have taken their organizations to new heights. Instead of seeing others' brilliance and flashes of inspiration as threats to be discouraged and rejected, Leaders invite these suggestions as opportunities for problem-solving and growth.

Leaders create environments that encourage others to contribute their viewpoints, which sometimes include contrarian opinions. While each team member has his or her weaknesses, Leaders are more concerned about their team members' capabilities. There is a time and place to address faults or areas where team members need to improve, and that is not during a group meeting.

In addition, a person's failure does not necessarily predict his or her potential. Thus, focusing on people's strengths and complimenting others is a Leader's default tendency.

Leaders identifying other Leaders among their ranks is a valued quality demonstrating one's ability to effectively head a team. But nurturing and developing a possible Leader's skills is of greater importance. All the potential in the world is useless unless its benefit is released. Positional Leaders identify team members who are respected and capable of growth. The wise Leader trains them and provides them with resources to flourish, such as access to key data, research, facilities, and personnel.

Such positional Leaders are expert at assessing their team members' capabilities and capacities. Some team members are skilled at coming up with innovative solutions. Others know how to take great ideas and turn them into tangible steps that lead to a measurable result. Still others can see how complex and ambitious objectives within a team or department play a role in the greater company or organization. And some within a team are adept at overseeing data and evidence to evaluate the direction a project is headed, as well as the degree to which it achieves its final objectives.

Once a project is declared complete, positional Leaders are often charged to present the results to others within the organization. When possible, we recommend dividing the presentation into parts. Each team member who championed a particular aspect of the project is then charged to describe the relevant topic.

Imagine a day when you, as a positional Leader, are presenting in front of your peers and superiors the successful result of a project your team has completed. You're excited to describe the outcome that exceeded your expectations, and you're confident those listening will be equally impressed.

But rather than play center stage in the presentation, you assume the role similar to that of a master of ceremonies. You bridge the gap between one presenter to another with introductory information. Meanwhile, each team member in charge of an aspect of the project brings it to life for the audience. This person presents with enthusiasm that reflects his or her expertise, deep understanding, and passion for the role he or she played. As you sit and listen to each presenter demonstrate Leadership, you are in awe of the talent around you and proud to have tapped into and developed Leaders within your organization.

As we described earlier, Leadership applies to individuals at any level of an organization. We do not ascribe Leadership with position, C-level or otherwise. When positional Leaders free and encourage others to take calculated risks, they harness the best of what their team members offer. Leaders push their teams in two simultaneous ways: They motivate and guide them to accomplish great things, and they identify and develop their individual talents and skills. By leveraging the Leadership qualities within their team members, Leaders improve their team's ability to do both of the preceding.

The Professional Mystique

Throughout society today, hierarchies are constantly being challenged. Formalities from previous generations are being dropped, and lines drawn between groups of people are being blurred. For instance, children were once taught to refer to grownups by their last names preceded by Mr., Mrs., or Miss. Today, children often refer to adults on a first-name basis.

We see how these widespread societal changes influence organizations and corporations. While the boss-employee structure and hierarchy are not going anywhere, the workplace setting has widely become more informal and relaxed. Some professions, such as most trial lawyers and Wall Street executives, still uphold strict dress codes, but the trend is toward more and not less informality. Casual Friday has morphed into casual every day for industries such as high tech, where Mark Zuckerberg's hoodies and Steve Jobs's black turtleneck and jeans were their workplace uniforms.

Positional leaders were once tucked away in their corner offices, sometimes perched above in their high-rise offices. Layers of corporate bureaucracy served as a barrier between leaders and followers. Separated by secretaries and human resources, positional leaders were sometimes well isolated from the rest of their workforce.

Nowadays, C-levels may be literally working side by side with their subordinates in their open office plans. Communication inevitably changes when positional leaders are not isolated from their organizations but instead are visible to them every day.

Common today and into the future are positional leaders celebrating the successes and grieving the failures within their organizations right alongside everyone else. Informality and frequent contact with subordinates within organizations mean that, for a positional leader, creating distance from those he or she is charged to lead is more difficult today. The positional leadership mystique of generations past has been replaced by one that sometimes leads to ambiguity between leaders and followers.

While workplace structures have changed, positional leaders today benefit from upholding aspects of the professional mystique. Open office settings may have broken down the physical barriers between leaders and followers. Leaders, however, benefit from maintaining psychological boundaries while maintaining authenticity. Being held ultimately responsible for the achievements and shortcomings of their organizations is the gift and burden of positional leaders.

While followers may be eager to celebrate a triumph, they may be equally quick to criticize a failure and assume no responsibility for it. Unfortunately, Leaders may not always be aware of how those around them handle bad news. They may act out in anger or aggression or even behave in ways that harm all you have worked to create within your organization.

This is one reason positional leaders gain from being prudent about their interactions. While you may feel that shedding your professional mystique with those within your organization is the sign of the transparency you promote, always consider the risk of doing so.

Openly sharing the private matters of you or others, trade secrets, personal ambition, connections, and contacts can work against you if a recipient of this information uses it irresponsibly or, even worse, to cause intentional damage. Ask experienced Leaders, and all will have stories where they were confident and comfortable about what they were revealing to a colleague, only to later regret doing so.

When in doubt, such as moments when the inner voice questions whether you should abstain or express something, follow the "less is more" approach to communication. This is particularly the case regarding delicate matters that have upset you. When describing these events, speak in general terms rather than risk saying too much about how someone offended or angered you.

Keep in mind that part of your role as Leader is to be a pillar of strength within your organization. To gain the respect and loyalty of your team, they must have confidence in you. For their sake and your own, you want to meet their high expectations. Although the concept of *authenticity* has seeped into corporate life, maintaining part of the bygone era of the professional mystique will serve you well.

Authenticity is often interpreted as an unfettered communication style. The words *vulnerability* and *transparency* also are often associated with authenticity. They both reflect a way to communicate that its adherents say makes the speaker more relatable and sparks empathy on the listener's part.

Leaders may show vulnerability and transparency by disclosing personal perspectives such as their insecurities, fears, and areas of weakness. Authenticity expressed in this way could motivate leaders to reveal aspects of their lives, such as their health status (from having mild stomach pain at the moment to battling a life-threatening heart condition) and their relationships (from a light argument with their teenage child that morning to an ugly, drawn-out divorce). They may express areas of professional weakness and inadequacy, such as describing a problem within the organization they are incapable of solving.

Authenticity, usually considered positive and genuine, is often pitted against insincerity, which is seen as negative and dishonest. We believe in a middle ground.

You don't have to tell others about your sex life or how much you can't stand your ex to be perceived as authentic. Nor need you describe the political party you support or your stance on controversial issues that make headline news. In fact, if the views you express will polarize more than unite your team, you are creating obstacles to realizing your vision for your organization. We also believe that a habit of expressing areas of professional weakness will harm your career over the long term. On the other extreme, maintaining manifest secrecy and distance from others can lead to them perceiving you as insincere.

Leadership requires tremendous strength both in your actions and in your words. As the character Frank Underwood said in the political-drama *House of Cards,* "There are two types of vice presidents: Doormats and matadors. Which do you think I intend to be?"[3] Matadors are admired for their ability to majestically and boldly redirect an angry bull that could

3 James Foley, director, *House of Cards,* season 2, chapter 16, February 14, 2014, Netflix.

easily kill them. These bullfighters meet their adversaries face-to-face, fully aware of the risks associated with their profession.

If a leader's actions are weak with the aura of a doormat, people won't respect his or her ideas. When faced with tough questions and reasoned criticism, Leaders defend their ideas rather than bend like a willow on a blustery day.

Weak leaders will inevitably make bad decisions that will thwart the achievement of their goals and ultimately impede their career advancement. When an otherwise capable leader uses words that express weakness, his adversaries and competitors will seek to use these to their advantage. Those who are ambitious, working toward meeting their goals, and advancing in their careers will constantly have others vying for their position or even anticipating their downfall.

Imagine you are surrounded by your adversaries and you openly describe an instance where you've reached a roadblock. Unable to solve a problem, you aren't optimistic about being able to effectively resolve it. You've now made yourself vulnerable in a negative way, similar to when a defense force lets down its guard and thereby is now open to enemy attack. Vulnerability in this sense is not the same as humility, which is generally considered a positive trait.

You want to make sure your version of authenticity isn't providing fodder to those who seek to identify your weaknesses and then use them at your cost and their benefit. Also, it's important to maintain credibility and respect among those who look to you for leadership.

You can have a full spectrum of resources functioning in your favor: a powerful and effective team working hard to earn support from those who will benefit your business, a marketing and public relations machine doing a stellar job highlighting the best your organization has to offer, and proprietary corporate practices that keep the company ahead of and distinct from your competitors. In sum, if you were a platoon, you would have a strong defense and offense that may, in fact, seem impenetrable.

Despite all this, however, you can still succumb to the forces working against you or waiting to take your place. Or because of all this, you can think you're safe, and this can lull you into complacency.

■ ■ ■

To say France was devastated after World War I is an understatement. Yes, it vanquished its neighboring enemy. Plus, considering Germany was a powerful nation state with a much larger population, French victory was an astonishing feat. But a large chunk of the "war to end all wars" was fought and won on French soil. This resulted in massive French casualties. In fact, an estimated 5 percent of the entire French population died—most of whom were soldiers sacrificing their lives in order to declare victory over Germany.

Following the war, the French government never wanted to experience such death and destruction of its people on its land again. Before satellites and modern missiles would result in the Reagan administration's Star Wars program and Israel's Iron Dome air defense system, France developed what was at the time the world's most advanced border protection network. This was preemptive defense technology on a scale unlike any other in human history. Named after André Maginot, a French war minister, the 280-mile series of massive protection structures would stretch along the border France shared with Germany, Luxemburg, and Belgium. Knowing that Germany was its biggest threat, the French government made the fortification between it and Germany the strongest part. If Germany sought to invade France, it would need to attack via Belgium to avoid the sturdiest section of the Maginot Line.[4]

In the event German forces invaded Belgium on its warpath toward France, the French government anticipated such a move would spark immediate action from Belgium's allies. This multinational military intervention would slow down German invasion, if not deter such a plan altogether. To execute its grand vision, France poured hundreds of billions of dollars' worth of concrete, steel, and cutting-edge engineering into the world's most advanced defense system. In the strongest stretch

4 History.com editors, "Maginot Line," History, updated October 4, 2022, https://www.history.com/topics/world-war-ii/maginot-line.

of the Maginot Line, its system was miles wide and included above- and below-ground fortifications.

On land were observation decks that would warn of an enemy on the move, minefields, rows of massive steel pillars designed to block tanks, machine gun stations, and dams and levees that, reminiscent of biblical accounts, could unleash floods to slow down the oncoming enemy.

Below ground were large, round, retractable gun emplacements, massive barracks that housed mess halls, dorms, hospitals, and recreation areas built to accommodate the five hundred thousand inhabitants charged to protect the French border. The series of underground structures was connected by a subway, power generator, and telecommunication system. The subterranean portion of the Maginot Line was self-contained with cold and hot water, air filtration that would protect inhabitants from gas attacks, and ample food supplies.

Praise for the Maginot Line spread across the country like a celebratory fever. It became a source of national pride. Newsreels promoted this military fortress of unparalleled and impressive scale. The French government proudly displayed the public works project that would keep its citizens safe and protected from its most fierce and aggressive neighbor.

The PR campaign gave French citizens peace of mind when the devastation of World War I was still in public memory. Optimism ran high thanks to the Maginot Line—to a degree that a troop drawdown seemed reasonable, given the country's near-impermeable border. The line's influence extended beyond France. Other countries saw its benefit and invested in similar technologies along their borders. Greece, Czechoslovakia, and even Germany (and on its border with France) installed their own versions of the French national defense.

In the years following World War I, tensions between France and Germany continued to build, justifying the construction of the border fortification. In May 1940, Hitler's army made its move to invade France. Rather than attempt to penetrate its border between France, the Germans swept through Belgium first. Unfortunately for France, its strategy to use

Belgium as a bulwark proved unsuccessful. A mere six weeks later, France fell to its neighboring rival in June.

In part, the Maginot Line performed as designed. German forces didn't invade France directly between their shared border, and Germany went around the fortification's strongest section. Since one of the objectives of the line was to protect France's border from Germany, in this regard, it worked. But its main purpose was to keep French citizens safe. In this regard, after hundreds of billions in taxpayer dollars and countless hours of labor, the result was one of history's most infamous public-works flops.

For Leaders, the Maginot Line is a cautionary tale that demonstrates their need to practice discretion and caution at all times. In recent history, we've seen countless high-profile leaders fall from grace after constructing their versions of the Maginot Line.

Powerful church heads with global audiences have been caught in financial and sex scandals. Beloved politicians seemed impervious to attack and criticism. But within the speed of one news cycle, they saw their clout crumble after being exposed of lies that diminished public safety and even resulted in death among the constituents they were elected to protect and serve.

Social media has exacerbated the need for Leaders to be prudent in their public and private lives. Tomorrow's Leaders will be scrutinized for social media content they posted or was posted about them during their young-adult years or even younger. With their lives digitized from their earliest memories, anything they say or do can be potential fodder for an attack—sometimes based on others' manipulating events or blatant deception.

We've seen today's public figures, such as politicians, judges, and presidential cabinet appointees, publicly questioned on C-SPAN for their actions decades ago, sometimes with disputable relation to the posts they seek. Fast-forward to today's young people applying for similar positions decades later. In addition to witness accounts, media articles, and testimony, they'll be held accountable for all social media platforms that have kept a forever-digital record of their existence.

Communication can be honest and sincere, which are the hallmarks of authenticity, while maintaining a professional mystique that includes communicating with prudence and caution. Holding both positions at the same time is often difficult and requires experience, wisdom, and discernment to do well.

Just as you would never recklessly reveal your organization's most coveted trade secrets, you benefit from carefully considering your words under all circumstances, rather than risk disclosing too much for the sake of being transparent. If authenticity means being honest and sincere, then it is one of the most important values a leader can uphold. Combine authenticity with the judicious boundaries required to maintain the professional mystique, and you have a wise communication strategy that will carry you through the future.

Fear, anxiety, stress, and anger are common to all humans. Leaders are no exception. When such intense emotions arise, Leaders have the responsibility to consider the consequences of their reactions to a greater extent than those who aren't under public scrutiny. Because they are called to exude a special charisma that inspires confidence and trust, they are held to a higher standard than most. Maintaining such an aura at this level of power requires constant wisdom. Finding trusted confidants, a so-called shoulder to cry on, is challenging but often provides a much-needed release valve.

We also believe that authenticity begins from the inside and extends outward. Described this way, authenticity starts with profound self-awareness. Leaders are responsible to know their weaknesses with precision. More than any other person within an organization, Leaders recognize their own blind spots and vulnerabilities.

For instance, if they realize they have a tendency to cry too often, drink too much, smoke, or engage in any number of activities that are harmful if done to excess, they figure out why and then go about creating change in themselves. Being authentic should never twist a person in knots. If it does, Leaders take charge to align their habits and actions with their values. Professional coaching, therapy, mentorship, self-reflection, and other means of receiving input from objective voices are examples of the many ways in which Leaders increase their self-awareness. From a deep understanding of oneself, Leaders have the tools to express themselves genuinely to others.

We've all witnessed when leaders are being publicly insincere. The most well-known cases are high-profile politicians whose attempts at authenticity are often expressed by way of consultants and advisors. This demonstrates the difference between maintaining the leadership mystique versus upholding a phony façade. The two may seem the same, but they are completely different.

Political leaders may speak in a regional accent that matches their listeners' but not their real language background. They may dress down or up in hopes to be more relatable to their audience. You may see an old politician pander to younger voters by making youth-culture references (such as to pop music and slang considered cool) and aligning themselves with celebrities and influencers. They may hide behaviors that put their positions at risk, such as smoking, drugs, and sex. Or they may refuse to disclose their genuine position on controversial and relevant subjects that could offend their constituents.

In 1988, Michael Dukakis and George Bush were running against each other for president. Dukakis was a strong candidate for the Democratic Party. One salient criticism leveled against him was that the Massachusetts governor was soft or lacked experience on issues of national security and foreign policy. The other side also argued that Bush worked alongside Reagan, who had what it took to win the Cold War.

As a way to counter this critique, Dukakis's team arranged for him to give a campaign speech at a General Dynamics facility. The company was a major US defense contractor and manufacturer of the $4.3 million M1A1 tank. The stop was intended to show that the Massachusetts governor was tough when it came to national defense and had the bravado to be the commander in chief.[5]

Dukakis would deliver remarks and ride atop an eight-foot tank in

5 Josh King, "Dukakis and the Tank: The Inside Story of the Worst Campaign Photo Op Ever," Politico, November 17, 2013, https://www.politico.com/magazine/story/2013/11/dukakis-and-the-tank-099119/.

front of reporters. Already, his team was concerned that the five-foot-eight-inch candidate would look weak and tiny compared to the eight-foot-high armored behemoth. Then there was the helmet.

While General Dynamics required him to wear it for safety reasons, combined with the large "Mike Dukakis" nametag printed on it, it ran the risk of looking contrived and artificial, the governor appearing more like a kid living out his boyhood fantasy of riding a tank than a credible candidate for the world's most powerful post.

Despite these misgivings, the potential pluses to the photo op—showing his solidarity with the military and the importance he placed on national defense—outweighed the possible minuses.

While the entire event went smoothly, it left him vulnerable to attack. And, boy, did the Bush campaign eviscerate the candidate! The scathing ad campaign used the tank footage from Dukakis's stop to mercilessly mock him.

Team Dukakis scheduled the tank ride to show that he had what it took to be a tough leader—including of the armed forces. One could interpret the short video as a harmless tank ride. But the Bush campaign seized on this opportunity to demonstrate Dukakis's insincerity. They used it to call out the presidential candidate's incompetence. The media panned the video for weeks, battering his campaign and showing him as a weak and out-of-touch leader. Some said Dukakis looked like Alfred E. Newman, the goofy, big-eared, buck-toothed *Mad* magazine character, riding atop the tank.

As cited by Politico, the narration of one ad summarizes how the Bush campaign used Dukakis's tank appearance to attack its opponent: "Michael Dukakis has opposed virtually every defense system we develop. He opposed new aircraft carriers. He opposed antisatellite weapons." It goes on to include other military operations he refused to support. Questioning his ability to lead the country, it ends with "America can't afford that risk."[6] Authenticity was used as a campaign weapon. Specifically, the

---

6 Josh King, "Dukakis and the Tank: The Inside Story of the Worst Campaign Photo Op Ever," Politico, November 17, 2013, https://www.politico.com/magazine/story/2013/11/dukakis-and-the-tank-099119/.

Bush team successfully convinced voters of Dukakis's insincerity. His tank appearance was masterfully described as false political posturing intended to offset Dukakis's genuine disdain for US defense. The Bush team fed and fomented characterizations of Dukakis as a weak and inexperienced candidate who didn't have what it took to defeat our foreign adversaries.

One minor and seemingly harmless campaign appearance turned into fodder to aggressively pounce on a political foe. The negative ad is referenced as one of the most effective political attacks in marketing history. It used an event staged by the candidate's team itself and put him on the defense. While not the reason for Dukakis's unsuccessful bid, it fueled the Bush team's winning and ruthless campaign strategy.

Years later, President Obama was given a navy football helmet and was asked to put it on. He refused. "You don't put stuff on your head if you're president. That's Politics 101," he said.

The professional mystique doesn't mean you are aloof and cold to the point where you're viewed as uncaring and perhaps intimidating. You do, however, want to continually remind yourself that being a Leader means you're a role model.

Part of that responsibility is to motivate others to release their professional potential within an organization. One way to do so is through your inspiring example, which earns others' trust in your abilities. As intelligent social beings, we seek to have confidence in others, and one of your roles as Leader is to engender this response.

Imagine a solider on the battlefield during deadly combat. Desperate for guidance, he turns to his commanding officer.

"Don't look at me! I don't have the answers," his superior tells him.

You could argue that this admission is an example of authenticity. But it is one that would benefit from a big dose of wise discretion. Leaders are respected for both the matters of the heart they disclose and what they don't reveal, especially insecurities about a particular decision or course of action.

The professional mystique for future Leaders means maintaining the boundary between leader and follower under a workplace environment that is increasingly more informal and flexible. Maintaining boundaries under these circumstances isn't easy, but doing so is part of earning others' respect. When they have confidence in your role as Leader, you increase the likelihood that they'll remain loyal and committed to your organization's mission.

Summary

During a snowy day, two NFL teams fought toward victory. Millions across the country watched the game from the warmth of their homes—far from this outdoor battle's icy midwestern setting. By the end of the matchup between two of the toughest teams in professional football, players on both sides had war-worn expressions clearly showing they had left nothing behind. Their hours of head-to-head combat on a slippery, snow-covered field heightened the danger of a game already known for its ruthless physicality. Victory was hard earned through the very end and could have easily gone to either team in this matchup of equally talented titans.

The winners, while weary and drained, had a second-wind adrenaline rush fueled by the thrill of triumph. The brothers in combat knocked helmets with each other, hugged it out, and whooped like warriors who had just vanquished a fierce enemy.

Some younger players from the winning team saw the snow on the field as a chance to have some sophomoric fun in front of the cameras. They lay on the frosty white that blanketed the grass and swung their arms and legs like windshield wipers. The snow angels they made were reminiscent of boyhood antics on a school playground. Meanwhile, the winning quarterback's wide smile, bright eyes, and unbridled hollers expressed that he, too, was filled with just as much elation. But rather than indulge in childlike impulses, the quarterback remained upright and proud—like a lieutenant celebrating victory with his platoon.

Was there anything objectionable about his teammates celebrating in their own way? Not at all. They were, after all, indulging in harmless fun, simply letting loose after hours of intense athletic combat. But here the quarterback demonstrated the professional mystique. Far from stoic or indifferent about the win, he expressed his excitement while upholding the unspoken code of conduct expected of a popular and respected player. He was a role model and the most high-profile face of the multibillion-dollar NFL team.

In the next chapter, we'll explore how Leaders effectively tap into their power, which is the fuel that drives their high achievement.

Chapter 7

POWER AT ITS BEST

IN THE BOTTOM of the ninth, Luke made his way to home plate. At nine years old, he was the youngest on the team. As he went to bat, he visualized the many times he had practiced for this moment. While he had drilled with his teammates and on his own, refining his technique, no amount of work could have prepared him for the pressure he felt right now.

He warmed up by throwing his shoulders back and swinging at imagined pitches. His team was behind, and losing the game seemed likely. Luke's performance would determine whether his team would have to walk off the field in defeat or celebrate victory.

The pitcher stood in front of him on the mound, wound up, and rocketed the ball toward Luke. He swung. Strike one. Luke shuffled his feet to reset his mind and then held steady as the next pitch zoomed by him. Ball one. He tapped his bat on the plate. The third ball came and . . . strike two.

"You've got this, Luke!" "C'mon, son!" he heard from the stands.

He tightened his little hands on the bat, buoyed by the encouragement he heard in the distance. The ball came streaming across home plate, and Luke didn't react. Ball two.

Then came another one.

Crack! The bat struck and shot the ball through the air. The crowd let out a collective gasp as it flew across the field. As Luke circled the diamond and touched home plate, he saw his teammates and onlookers in the bleachers jumping up and down. He heard the cheers from the dugout and crowd. And he felt a surge of adrenaline that fueled his sprint.

While still in shock over his feat, Luke suddenly felt a chill run through his body. His teammates had dumped the cooler's contents on him to declare victory. Drenched in ice water and pride, Luke looked at his family who were in the stands. His smile matched the excitement they felt after witnessing him reach this proud moment.

In an instant, the boy knew what it felt like to be a hero. Achieving the game-winning run caused his self-esteem to soar. That towering accomplishment gave Luke, at a young age, a tangible experience of what possessing personal power felt like.

■ ■ ■

We Americans are obsessed with individual power. Personal power is a key characteristic of being able to live a purpose-driven life. Considering the heights we've achieved as a nation throughout our short and exceptional history, our preoccupation with power makes sense. An innate inner will within our population, combined with the fertile Land of Opportunity, has resulted in humankind's greatest accomplishments.

From the TV series we watch to the energy drinks we consume, power—where it comes from and how to increase it—is a national theme embedded in our everyday lives. As it relates to Leadership, power is the capacity to influence the behavior of others or the course of events.

Power is often described as negative. *Power hungry, powermonger,* and *power trip* are common descriptors for archetypes such as the main villain in a superhero comic, the tyrannical and heartless boss in a movie, or the malevolent president in a political novel. We've seen countless real-world examples of this Darth Vader and Cruella de Vil version of power. Thus we will not focus on its dark side in this chapter. Rather, we'll explore the positive connection between Leadership and power and how to develop and use it effectively.

A strong sense of purpose motivates Leaders in their pursuit of excellence. With power, a Leader's purpose takes on great significance. Lasting societal improvements, influential inventions, and positive disruption within industries entrenched in the status quo are three major results of the power-purpose combination. Thus, leaders benefit by learning to exert, with comfort and skill, the power that accompanies positional leadership. In this chapter, you'll learn how Leaders harness power to meet their greatest objectives.

The Origins of Power

Healthy self-esteem rooted in one's accomplishments forms the foundation of personal power. These include even seemingly insignificant experiences we've had from a young age. Learning to walk, read, and ride a bike are early examples of accomplishments that grow bigger over time. Young children develop their sense of worth by being exposed to experiences that provide them with growth opportunities. But failure to master or overcome these situations can have the opposite effect. They can stifle a person's development.

Our early life experiences influence how we view the world and what we perceive as right or wrong. Children measure their value based on the importance others place on them. When they are nurtured and cared for, they learn what others expect of them. In turn, they understand what they must fulfill in order to excel as a valuable member of their community or family. The opposite is true as well. Neglect and abuse may result in young people believing little is expected of them.

Children have an innate sense of self-control that increases or diminishes as they learn to deliver on the expectations placed on them. These early experiences influence whether children view their immediate environment and the greater world they live in as a positive, supportive place or a negative, hostile one.

As young people become adults, they build on the experiences of their formative years to develop their power. Unfortunately, social forces have hijacked their ability to develop the skills necessary to have the high levels of self-control Leadership requires. Technological advances—from smartphones and tablets to gaming—have a bright and dark side. The consequences of too much screen time have resulted in less in-person engagement. The socialization (or lack thereof) this brings about in a young person's developing mind causes difficulties in maintaining focus and attention, in creating the discipline necessary to organize thoughts and then execute a plan, and in developing impulse control.

Adults who effectively use power have a high degree of self-discipline that, in most cases, they developed years before. They learned early on that the ability to influence others starts with self-control that sets them apart from their peers.

Power and Self-Control

The common images describing what self-control looks like are of Mahatma Gandhi calmly guiding an entire nation to independence and the Dalai Lama as a peaceful leader exiled from his native country.

But beyond displaying external calm, self-control is a force that permeates a Leader's whole identity and influences an array of behaviors. The actions of people who have mastered it follow their intentions, which are guided by their purpose. A Leader's self-control demonstrates itself in the mundane, as well as the extraordinary. From personal finance, dietary decisions we make, and whom we associate with on a daily basis to solving major workplace crises, self-control is woven through a Leader's life. Leaders practice it in their diets and drinking habits and relationships.

Self-control is not a personality trait that is turned on or off like a light switch. It is not harnessed only when necessary. Rather, it's part of a Leader's DNA.

We see people who lack self-control at all levels of society. CEOs and teenagers enter drug rehab. Church pastors and public school teachers are caught in sex scandals. Politicians and civil servants steal public money. Thus self-control in all aspects of one's life is not a requisite for professional success. Leadership extends beyond one's job title, career accomplishments, station in life, and income. Leaders' professional and personal lives overlap more so today than before smartphones and social media were common. A bad decision or mistake in one sphere influences the other. Leaders who practice self-control in all areas have high-achievement-driven, well-balanced lives and decrease the likelihood of making poor decisions and errors.

Self-control is calculated behavior that takes many forms. This is why the common examples of self-control are insufficient. While Mahatma Gandhi leading a mass protest is an example of it, another Leader's impassioned and energetic speech can be equally self-controlled. When Leaders manifest a particular set of behaviors to their audience that aligns with their purpose, this is an example of demonstrating self-control.

Self-Control and Communication

Young, rookie leaders may use forceful, aggressive communication to express their positional muscle within the organization. Meanwhile, strong, confident, and mature Leaders describe what they want and encourage and even teach others to develop their own path to achieve the organization's objectives.

Self-control forms the foundation of effective communication. Leaders modulate their outward behavior based on setting and context. In a team meeting, Leaders know when to speak and argue a point vigorously and when to listen to opposing viewpoints.

You can be confronted by an angry group of employees challenging you over the termination of one of their coworkers. You can be confronted by a newspaper reporter over a statement you made. Or your point of view can be vigorously argued against and harshly condemned. Meanwhile, confidentiality clauses mean you can't tell your staff details about the sexual harassment investigation that resulted in the termination. You don't have time to explain why the accusation levied on you is a lie. And you are privy to facts and information you aren't allowed to disclose to your stakeholders that would otherwise immediately get them on your side. But under all three circumstances, you're still required to respond.

What is the best way to address the dissatisfied or angry mob, whether in person or on social media? There is no one approach that works every time. Sometimes silence is best. Other times, deferring the topic of discussion to a future date to allow tempers to cool is the wise move. In other instances, a passionate, assertive, or even aggressive response may be the most appropriate, as long as it is controlled.

Imagine that a photo of a state governor with his brow furrowed, pointing his finger at the camera, circulates on the web. The photo was taken during a televised political debate where the governor admonished his opponent in front of the cameras. The otherwise calm and steady Leader consciously chose this moment to express his outrage. His anger was calculated and purposeful.

Self-control touches every aspect and skill associated with Leadership. Leaders are guided by being the most authentic versions of themselves. Thus, if they believe strongly in something, they stand behind it vigorously. They express themselves honestly and demonstrate how they seek to work with others, upholding trust and transparency. This can be communicated loudly or quietly. In either case, it is done with discipline and control.

When leaders lose control, often expressed through yelling, profanity, or even disrespectful words and actions, they lose credibility, no matter how legitimate the grounds are for their outrage. Like a child throwing a temper tantrum, they may impulsively blurt out whatever comes to mind.

While social media has loosened rules against communicating with expletives, most Leaders should refrain from using them as much as possible. One reason is that F-bombs and other four-letter words may offend listeners who would otherwise agree with your points. Another reason is you never know how someone will interpret your words that are impossible to take back. Thus, err on the side of caution.

Leaders understand that on a daily basis countless factors are beyond their control—and many of these pose a huge threat to their organizations. They direct immense energy and focus on how and to what extent they are able to control the situation. They know that the power of their position means their self-control influences those around them to a degree that others do not. When most would cave under pressure, this mastery of self-control allows Leaders to remain levelheaded under difficult and sometimes downright hostile circumstances. By practicing it when faced with adversity, they avoid making emotionally driven snap judgments and impulsive decisions that can result in terrible mistakes. Self-control increases the likelihood that Leaders maintain the patience and clarity necessary to evaluate a complex problem and objectively listen to what others have to say.

Despite their skill, Leaders make mistakes. Every day, Leaders are placed in difficult situations. They're solving problems within their organizations and being the target of media and public scrutiny—all while maintaining a long-term vision. Under this constant pressure, making the wrong decision or saying the wrong thing is inevitable. All Leaders can recall a time when, during the intensity of the moment, they succumbed to emotions or the weaker aspects of their character, which resulted in an action they later regretted. These are key points of contemplation where Leaders commit to learning from their mistakes and about their own flaws and limitations. They use the power of self-reflection and improvement to make better future decisions.

Masterful communication is equal parts what is stated and explicitly expressed and what is unstated and implied. Effectively balancing both separates the rookies from the masters. In addition, Leaders acknowledge that positive and constructive communication forms part of the power they use to accomplish challenging and ambitious tasks.

Men and women with a high sense of personal power understand cause and effect. They recognize that work directed toward a worthwhile task based on wise decision-making will result in a healthy outcome. Using their understanding of cause and effect, they skillfully organize their thoughts. Every activity requires a clear view of all necessary steps. From the simplest to most complex tasks, Leaders organize their activities in a masterfully sequenced and reasonable manner. This is one example of the higher order thinking that Leaders possess.

Throughout history, men and women have unleashed their inner Leader and have turned the most radical and incomprehensible dreams into groundbreaking products and services, as well as political, social, and religious movements. But without translating their dreams into a straightforward plan comprising clear steps, their grand ambitions would have remained stuck in the realm of the imagination.

Potential Leaders benefit from identifying and acting early upon their inner drive. Throughout their formal educational years, they have countless extracurricular activities and academic experiences that will develop their abilities and provide them with the tools they need throughout their professional lives. The formal learning through coursework and informal learning through activities outside the classroom provide young people the experiences necessary to discover their purpose, passions, strengths, and weaknesses.

Keep in mind that age does not necessarily limit a person's Leadership potential. You'll find examples of people who have discovered and developed their talents later in life. Anna Mary Robertson Moses, later known as Grandma Moses, began painting at seventy-eight years old. She went on to become famous the world over for her depictions of rural American life, continuing to refine her craft a few months before her passing at 101 years old. While exceptions such as Grandma Moses exist, the earlier we begin on our ambitious path, the more time we give ourselves to develop the discipline, confidence, and skills necessary to achieve greatness.

As Leaders throughout history have demonstrated, each practical step moves them closer to the outcome they've envisioned. Unfortunately, we see a great tragedy among young potential Leaders today: They may have the vision, but too often they lose hope because they lack the guidance or courage or both necessary to complete fundamental tasks.

Expressing one's vision clearly and effectively, staying steadfastly focused, and implementing an action plan are essential for potential Leaders to gain positional power and lead a life driven by immense purpose. Human civilization's greatest men and women are those who embrace lifelong learning, gain wisdom through trial and error, and never give up. Combined, these three characteristics imbue Leaders with the knowledge required to effectively manage and use power.

In the following section, you'll learn the building blocks of developing the kind of power that will separate you from the pack.

Peer Power

Leaders require a worldview that provides them with the skills and talent necessary to overcome the many obstacles they'll face and successfully navigate toward the numerous destinations they'll travel. It is during this journey where Leaders realize the importance of understanding and managing power.

From our earliest years, we see the power dynamic play out within our peer groups. On the playground, some children identify themselves as leaders, while the rest follow. In make-believe games about war, the young leader will take the role of general, directing soldiers; in playing house, the emerging leader will play the role of parent guiding children; or in a Medieval fantasy, kings or queens will rule over their land. These young leaders set the agenda for the behaviors expected of their peers.

Within a traditional school setting, the campus population dictates the pool of individuals students can associate with. Those who associate themselves with high achievers who positively influence others will increase the likelihood that their actions and behaviors will align with those of their peer group. The opposite is true as well. Those who align themselves with low achievers and peers who negatively influence others will increase the likelihood that they too will manifest similar characteristics. In either case, people are judged by the associations they maintain.

Once we graduate from high school, we have a wider group from which to select our peers. But the same tendency continues. From college to our professional years, we are judged by the institutions (such as universities), organizations (such as social, vocational, and networking groups), and individuals (friends, colleagues, and mentors) we engage with. These are examples of the basic form of grown-up power, which is achieved through association.

Leaders, particularly those early in their career trajectories, benefit from considering this aspect of power. As they plan how they'll advance in their professions, it is important they take time researching the activities that will serve them well. With countless options available to chart the course to their ideal version of work, there are many activities that can thwart or accelerate career advancement. Thus through thorough investigation, they will increase the likelihood of making the right long-term decisions.

Our peers and peer groups offer powerful connections and ongoing opportunities for continuous learning. They allow us to participate in new activities and develop networks. The people we meet have the potential to provide support during the career challenges we face. We can turn to them to help us solve problems, support our causes, and improve our ability to determine when to take risk—and as we advance, the stakes and their consequences become greater. The quality of the individual or group is more important than the number of men and women we interact with.

Expert Power

In advanced societies like ours, we have multiple means to quantify expertise. Degrees, certifications, licenses, and credentials are common measures of skill and subject-matter mastery. You can have a bachelor's, master's, or doctorate degree that designates you a professor, engineer, lawyer, or physician.

You can have a certification that qualifies you to draw blood (phlebotomist), teach (state-issued credential), work in a lab (licensed technician), cut hair (cosmetologist), or drive a semitruck (commercial driver's license). For some people, reaching this level of achievement marks a mission accomplished and a dream fulfilled. For others, it is a hard-earned leap forward that opens doors for upward professional and social mobility.

While many people have the requisite training to provide a service, we distinguish this from the level of expertise Leaders possess. We define a Leader's superior expertise as being beyond the realm of technical knowledge.

Leaders' knowledge and experience set them apart from a similarly trained or qualified individual. They have a higher level of thinking that gives them the ability to do things others cannot. They are able to avoid or diminish downsides, despite the often bold and big risks they take. When faced with crushing defeat, they have the resources, talent, and will to overcome it.

Confidence through expert knowledge contributes to their sought-after decision-making ability. Whereas others may be resistant to move forward with a particular task, experts know their skill set gives them the ability to contribute in a specific way. Their talent presents opportunities to participate in discussions and planning. These are critical to completing tasks that maintain the momentum they need to move forward with their ambitious goals.

Demonstrating their expertise within their organizations is a common way Leaders advance within their careers. This separates them from other similarly qualified individuals. Yes, all experts have mastered a certain domain. A person may be a foremost geologist, and his years of study and research qualify him to find the best sites to drill for natural resources. But this is not Leadership. A geologist who is a Leader has a level of knowledge extending far beyond academic training.

Leaders garner resources and execute the processes to hire, train, manage, guide decision-making and policy, execute a plan, and create positive and dramatic change within their organizations. Some physicians are foremost cancer doctors, while even fewer are the heads of prestigious medical schools' oncology departments.

While others may have more technical knowledge, Leaders demonstrate expertise in their ability to bring information together in usable and practical ways for their organizations. They share techniques and approaches that improve collaboration within their company's teams. These can be a Leader's significant and extraordinary contribution that earns others' confidence and trust.

Leaders increase their expertise through a lifelong commitment to growth that moves far beyond formal study. They frequently volunteer for special assignments such as writing curriculum, developing a company's work-from-home plan, serving on committees to search for new company locations, or reallocating resources. Early in the Leadership journey, they may act as an organization's ambassador responsible to give tours to visitors. Participation in these assignments provides Leaders with a deep understanding of an organization's critical functions and allows them to identify strengths and weaknesses. Volunteering gives Leaders privileged access to high-level professionals and areas that most never see. The knowledge and experience they gain from these exclusive opportunities are beyond what would otherwise be possible.

An emerging Leader never knows what part of a special assignment can open future doors. For example, you may be asked to serve on a committee and initially hesitate because of the time your service will require. But you decide to say yes. One day, you are requested to attend a board meeting. Afterward, you are invited to a board's executive session. This opportunity to be among your organization's top leaders in a small setting is an encounter you would have otherwise missed out on entirely.

Your participation in a special assignment may provide new experiences you'll add to your skill set. Perhaps you're holding press conferences, conducting interviews, or coordinating important events. Leaders say yes to more responsibility when they see that it aligns with their ambitious vision. Rather than fear taking on responsibility that involves learning a new skill set, they research and develop what is necessary to fulfill their duties. Overpreparing for a task at hand is a Leader's tendency, and this transfers to their special assignment.

Participating in formal and informal professional networks is another way Leaders build upon their expertise. Formal networks include trade associations related to a particular expertise, such as the National Society of Professional Engineers, the Screen Actors Guild, the American Medical Association, and other trade unions, as well as networking groups such as the Rotary Club, Kiwanis, Young Presidents' Organization, and Entrepreneurs' Organization. These often provide training and collaborative opportunities.

Leaders take this knowledge and apply it to groups within their organization or the entire company itself. Because Leaders have a deep understanding of their organization's vision, including its culture, they know what new information they gain from networking groups will best apply to their teams.

Positional Leaders share their expertise. As champions for their organization's vision, they realize that collaboration is one of the greatest assets in today's most influential companies. Leaders are sought-after for their ability to redesign divisions, departments, or entire organizations for them to grow now and into the future. They are relentlessly focused simultaneously on today and tomorrow and always open to change direction, dramatically if need be, in order to continually elevate their organizations to new heights.

Purposeful Power

The driving force behind a Leader's accomplishment is purpose. Leaders know their purpose well, and it's what compels them to use their intellect, energy, and focus to practice Leadership. When confronted with adversity, as well as adversaries, their purpose pushes them to passionately fight rather than flee. They dig deep within themselves and tap into the grit, perseverance, and commitment required to overcome the major obstacles that come with high achievement.

Leaders have earned the authority and responsibility they hold through developing and then executing a purposeful plan. At first glance, having such an intentional plan seems like a fundamental and unextraordinary prerequisite—a simple expectation for all leaders. But this erroneous belief assumes purposeful planning is the same as merely accomplishing a task. For example, an employee needs to submit a multimedia presentation at day's end for a pending video conferencing meeting. Thus, his purpose for that day is to complete all the slides. This is not a purposeful plan.

Rather, a purposeful plan is a series of tasks and projects (which may include multimedia presentations) that Leaders coordinate to accomplish a grand objective. Leaders understand the role each task and project play toward bringing about the ambitious and measurable outcomes they are inspired to achieve. A Leader's purpose-driven outcomes cause increasingly greater results. These accomplishments call attention to the Leader's ability. Over time, his or her worth becomes known throughout the organization. At some point, this renown reaches a critical level, and the Leader's bright light ignites the potential of those around him or her. This engagement of others is how Leaders assume greater and greater power.

A Leader alone cannot assess an organization's problems, create processes to address them, and then solve them. By persuasively engaging others to eagerly participate in their cause, Leaders produce status quo–breaking outcomes that form part of their legacy. Having stakeholders fully invested in implementing the process plays an important role when hitting obstacles. Problems arise, no matter how thoroughly you've anticipated them. Your stakeholders will be motivated to play a role in course correcting when they are as eager to reach the desired outcome as you are.

While major accomplishments are moments to celebrate, their big impact means they are risky—sometimes jaw-droppingly so. Thus, the dark side to high accomplishment is epic failure, which is always a possibility.

Seeking the safety of underperformance versus the possible consequences associated with big ambition can seem like the wisest move. After all, epic failures often become the target of news and social media criticism.

But valuing security and comfort over insecurity and discomfort can result in mediocre professional performance. So fearing failure should never be the reason to avoid taking risk.

Unfortunately, a consequence of being afraid of failure is setting the so-called chicken goal, which is one that is easily achieved. The accomplishment bar is purposely set low to avoid having a failure in one's repertoire. Chicken goals duck the grueling persistence that high-impact achievement requires. They allow leaders to stay clear from being rejected, ridiculed, and scrutinized by others. By setting them, leaders don't have to win over skeptics and naysayers, let alone persuade them to allocate their time and skills to an ambitious cause. Chicken goals are about short-term gratification: feeling a sense of confidence right away, placing greater importance on goal accomplishment than on its real impact, and mitigating risk to the point where little changes.

Here, we see an example of the broader fake news trend within organizations. Evaluating data is key to driving solid decisions. But it can be used to make a chicken goal seem loftier than it is. And it can easily be manipulated to generate the sought-after outcome. It can be used to confirm and thus move forward with terrible plans. Data can also serve to distract when amassing facts becomes the goal. This may result in avoiding making true, positive, and lasting change.

When goal-setting is authentic, purposeful, and focused on being objective and honest at all costs, data have a higher likelihood of accurate interpretation. Data that are interpreted with an open mind and expressed clearly to all stakeholders play a critical role in any project. When this fundamental understanding of data is upheld, Leaders can focus on honing the subjective skills of listening, communication, and observation.

Both Leaders and their counterparts may put forth chicken goals. But for Leaders, these are secondary goals necessary to reach big, ambitious ones. Rather than results to be proud of, they are essential yet small steppingstones.

Leaders decrease risk through their careful and thorough analysis. They work toward challenging goals with noble purpose. When faced with a difficult problem to solve, accurately identifying the change that needs to be made is the biggest challenge. This is why so many leaders and their teams become bogged down—and waste precious time; they misidentify a problem and deal with symptoms rather than address the problem's root cause. Similar to hikers who take a wrong turn and then trek for miles along the wrong path, solving a secondary problem, rather than the primary one, or failing to discern the real concern outright, results in both lost opportunity and squandering time that cannot be recouped.

On the other hand, Leaders are adept at correctly identifying issues and then implementing the proper process to resolve them. To do this, Leaders require a deep understanding of the necessary procedures, which allows them to avoid breakdowns that often plague poorly executed procedures.

A method of evaluation is also essential to have in place before implementing a process. This includes a means to gather data, which are constantly used to inform and guide the process. When evidence demonstrates the need to make improvements or changes, Leaders will trigger an action plan they've developed ahead of time that illuminates the path forward. In other words, rather than rely on improvisation, they have a guide that provides instructions on how they will course correct efficiently.

Agility, flexibility, and adapting to change rapidly and effectively in the midst of fulfilling one's purpose lessen the chance of failed outcomes and increase the likelihood of spectacular results. Skillfully implementing improvements mid-process demonstrates your robust oversight. Leadership reaches its fullest potential when you've mastered the art of having a clear purpose that governs action.

Accomplishments: Measures of Achievement

A Leader's professional journey is one of exceptional performance, with success the default and rare instances of failure over a Leader's career. Excellence and working to a high level creating maximum positive impact in an organization are part of Leaders' daily lives. They are constantly striving to realize the very best outcome of whatever endeavor they pursue.

While external recognition and reward are associated with high-profile, high-achievement Leaders, their primary drive comes from within. External organizations that confer honorary degrees, write positive articles about Leaders, or invite them to join boards seek to both commend individuals and use them as examples to inspire others to greatness.

For Leaders, these platforms help them reach a wide audience. Such external praise draws attention to your talents and persona. As a result, people want to know more about you, they want to learn your backstory, and they want to be like you. But in some cases, they want to compete head-to-head with you—ensuring your challenges never end.

The reward for high accomplishment is more accomplishment. So be prepared to extend your ambition. Your track record of success will open doors for you that you may have never considered. This part of the Leader's journey is full of memorable surprises that can take you around the world and to destinations you would have never otherwise traveled.

In today's connected world, assume that people you meet want to learn about you. From a chance interaction with you while waiting in line to a video conference of you describing your expertise, once people learn about you, they use their search engines to discover more and thereby create their version of you. Unfortunately, it may not be exactly the one you want them to have. Rather than yield to online overlords to dictate who you are, where you've been, and what you do, take control over your digital persona. Using the internet tools within your control, present and communicate a message that aligns with your values and vision.

Instead of viewing this exposure as a burden, realize that your visibility will only increase over time, given your future achievements and the greater role of technology in our lives. Today, positional Leaders have no choice to hide from the public eye. They are accountable to their organizations and to those who see them on their phones and desktops. Managing this intense recognition well requires careful planning and support.

Staying updated with current technology supports Leaders' management of their organization's public profile. It also improves the image they project as their organization's head. Being well informed and actively participating in social media allows Leaders to better manage and control their public persona. It also provides an excellent opportunity to create a digital legacy of their accomplishments.

By seeking the guidance of individuals who are further along than you in the use of technology, such as social media, you and your digital reputation may greatly benefit. As is the case with any endeavor, reaching out to mentors, coaches, or even colleagues on a formal or informal basis is a wise move. These trustworthy and generous individuals can provide small doses of information on an as-needed and infrequent basis. By seeking the input and advice of others, you'll have an objective perspective when you're considering your options, evaluating one action versus another, and determining the direction you will take.

Maintain a long-term perspective while being firmly rooted in the present. Your current role is preparing you for your next. In the present, you are creating your real-time reputation. In the future, these accomplishments will form part of your long-term legacy. In the present, learn to skillfully share the accomplishments of you, your team, and your organization. In this way, you are taking control of how you present your message rather than leaving it up to others. No one understands better than you what you and your team have done.

Developing personal marketing materials is one way to take control. For example, when you are asked to publicly speak, event coordinators will often ask, "Can you send me a short bio?" Oftentimes, if it is well written, they will copy and paste what you wrote word for word into their event marketing collateral.

Companies with marketing budgets frequently generate press releases to publicize a new CEO hire, a product launch, facilities expansion, or the buyout of a competitor. If compelling and well written, news outlets frequently take this content and publish it on their own websites. Cash-strapped news organizations and their editors are often relieved to receive free and quality content that they can repurpose without spending a penny.

Your personal marketing material can be equally effective in providing you and your organization with free publicity. Thus, distribute impeccably written content with the understanding your exact words may be reproduced. This must include content that has no spelling or grammatical errors. It should be well organized, concise, and aesthetically attractive. Anything less, and your prospective client or audience will question your credibility.

Find an objective person with solid language skills that you'll regularly rely on to review your material. Throughout their careers, Leaders have seen countless job applications and personal marketing materials of others that have typos or are poorly written. These, along with the prospect of the authors being taken seriously by the organization, are often tossed in the trash. If candidates cannot produce high-level documents when seeking positions directly affecting their livelihoods, then it is unlikely they will consistently reach an acceptable standard in their day-to-day work.

Throughout doctors' offices today, you'll find multiple racks filled with content for you to read. While magazines have been commonplace in waiting rooms, as a result of the doctors competing for patients, you'll frequently see materials about the physicians in the practice. This may be a simplified résumé written to a patient audience that describes a doctor's education and expertise, as well as includes light personal information such as marriage and family status and hobbies. You too would benefit from one page or less that describes your professional highlights, including awards and recognitions and organizations you participate in. By preparing this ahead of time, you'll have it ready when others request information about you.

Even if you aren't requested to provide particulars, offering to send them will be usually welcomed. If you are presenting at an event, provide your personal marketing material. When you have a meeting with a Leader in a one-on-one setting, such as when conducting an information-gathering interview, send a one-sheet description with your headshot ahead of time. For example, you are writing a book, and an expert has agreed to meet with you as part of your research. Prior to your interview, send your description. This will boost your credibility, and the photo will be appreciated to identify you when you both meet.

Part of your personal marketing materials may be your individual website or a portion on your organization's website about your role within it. Consider archiving video and audio content, including your public speaking events and interviews.

When it comes to personal marketing material, keep the content succinct to generate interest in the point you're making. One of your personal marketing material's principal objectives is to present who you are.

Keep track of the recognitions and awards granted in your chosen field, as well as beyond your industry. You or your organization or both may qualify to compete for local, national, and international prizes, recognition, and awards. Next, research the criteria for submitting an application and keep yourself updated. Guidelines can quickly change; thus you want to ensure you're providing exactly the information the group seeks in order to make your application as competitive as possible. One benefit of staying abreast of awards and recognitions is they help you understand what is valued in the job market in which you are seeking to grow.

Most important, be eager to take on new challenges. All Leaders have well-thought-out plans and have envisioned a clear path for themselves. While staying focused on your plan, also keep your eyes wide open to observe the magnificent world around you. By doing so, you are acting in accordance with your vision *and* realizing that amazing opportunities can improve your life, push you to the forefront of your career, and lead to more success.

Summary

Power, in its both malevolent and benevolent forms, fascinates us. From biblical stories to Hollywood blockbusters, we're obsessed with men and women who possess it.

A balanced expression of power is a Leadership requirement. As heads of organizations, we are under constant pressure to make wide-reaching and consequential decisions and scrutinized for outcomes to a degree that is rare in society. The pressures are enormous, and so is our requirement to always maintain self-control.

Social media has served to magnify our public visibility and cast an often-unforgiving shadow over our personal and professional lives. Yet rather than evade the spotlight, Leaders are charged to stand tall beneath it. We do so by our integrity, by our credibility, and by being master marketers of our organizations and ourselves.

A key component of Leadership is understanding one's purpose. This is what drives us to break the status quo when we deem it necessary to realize our vision. From there we set ambitious goals, take calculated risk, inspire others to become partners in our endeavor, and hold ourselves accountable for failures and successes according to the metrics we've established. Power is the key for Leaders to unlock the door to their current and future success.

In the next chapter, you'll learn how power used wisely is part of building expert teams. Through teamwork, Leaders accomplish more than is otherwise possible.

Chapter 8

EXPERT TEAMS

ENJOYED BY ALL generations, football is one of the most popular American pastimes. The sport excites families, friends, and communities of all kinds.

If you're meeting a stranger, bringing up football and a team's latest standings is a common conversation icebreaker. Fans love talking about a new quarterback's struggles, the team's recent loss, and new trades. From the team itself, the conversations often transition to its head coach. He's the one that receives credit for outstanding performance but bears the cutting criticism with a team's loss.

Fans share a strong bond with their favorite team. They revel in wearing its colors shown off in hats and jerseys. Loyalty runs deep and is handed down from generation to generation. Pregame tailgating is the height of celebration. Participants paint their faces, feast together, and gather the energy they'll unleash throughout game day. Over the course of the battle that plays out on the field, fans will shout with glee or moan with pain as the competition unfolds.

Football fans are the stakeholders who lend moral *and* financial support to their teams. The revenue they generate affects a team's quality. For teams falling short of expectations, improving outcomes is a coach's top priority. Replacing players in key positions is typically the first step. If that doesn't work, the next move may be replacing the head coach.

Experts operating in each position are key to winning. But consistently declaring victory requires more than this. Working together through developing chemistry is the secret sauce that brings individual talents together to produce extraordinary collective results. Each player supports his teammates through his expertise. Through the team's relentless practice and collaboration, stakeholders expect to see the individuals acting as one unit on game day.

How is it that some coaches create winning chemistry while others can't? Successful ones find top talent, work closely with professionals charged to recruit them, engage potential players, and then, once they're on board, create successful teams. Each step requires immense work and skill.

Coaches must ensure that, once players have joined the team, they continue to reach their potential and that new recruits experience high levels of motivation, passion, and joy, as well as understand the role they play in shaping an outstanding team. The team's success depends on the extent to which they mesh with others.

You'll find infinite parallels between exceptional football coaches and positional Leaders. Both are responsible for building and maintaining their teams. They respect their team members, provide them with opportunities for input, draw clear expectations, and hold them accountable. They also design intricate competitive strategies to achieve both short- and long-term positive outcomes. They do so by bringing alive what appears in a playbook in a way that yields consistent high performance.

Overcoming the competition, anticipating possible pitfalls and thereby evading them, and identifying the numerous factors that will determine a win or loss are part of competing at the highest level and essential to scoring major wins. Individuals who reach this level of Leadership are prized in any sector.

Creating Expert Teams

This is one of the most valued skills a Leader can have. In fact, it is a prerequisite. An expert team comprises a group of people working under a Leader's guidance. Within an expert team are individual and collective skills and talents. Each professional brings a specific knowledge, expertise, and skill set to the team. Collectively, all are highly self-motivated, committed, passionate about their work, open to learn from mistakes and grow, able to adapt to change, and disciplined. Together, they collaborate in order to meet common goals. They embody their organization's mission, vision, and values. Individually, they do their part to fulfill their responsibilities.

Those within and outside their organization recognize the creativity and the achievements of the expert team, as well as of the individuals within it. A team's integration is essential. The success of the whole is a result of each individual working together with his or her colleagues.

Recognition is one of the effects of the success of expert teams. It may be solicited, such as when a team applies for and then wins an award or prize. Or it may come through a team's drawing unsolicited attention, such as when hard work generates high-profile results. The flip side of praise is blame. In other words, when a team receives accolades, this attention will also inevitably attract criticism.

Leaders often find themselves the target of attacks that stem from misunderstandings and half-truths. They may be accused of making a particular decision based on their overinflated egos when, in fact, they were driven by more and different information outside of what others were privy to. When being the target of criticism, it's often difficult to maintain objectivity. Taking a defensive stance is far too easy. When hearing bad news, it's tough to remain calm and not wither under pressure. When your views are misrepresented and even lied about, it's hard to stay diplomatic and gracious rather than lash out uncontrollably.

Whatever the negative external input is, viewing all of it as fodder for learning, growing, and finding possibility no matter what can often feel like a bitter pill to swallow. But doing this well marks one of the hallmarks of Leadership. When you've arrived at this stage of professional development, you are prepared to inspire others to align their effort with the purpose shared by you, your expert team, and your organization. Others will take notice of your ability and seek out your expertise. At some point you may find yourself being called upon to mentor others.

Having an expert team is a prerequisite for Leadership. Without one, a leader will never be able to achieve success. Team building is one of the greatest joys of positional Leadership. It is challenging and demanding but also immensely fulfilling and rewarding. Working with creative, high-energy, talented, passionate, and loyal professionals can be one of the most thrilling and satisfying experiences in your career.

The enormous responsibility leaders carry in creating teams also has a dark side. Whereas the team receives accolades for successful outcomes, Leaders bear the brunt for poor results.

Without an expert team, one rarely successfully completes any work or project that breaks from the status quo and leads to major innovation. To build an expert team, Leaders set aside their egos. A Leader's ability to let go of his or her self-importance is essential to creating an excellent team that experiences exceptional outcomes. Letting go is a challenge for most Leaders who have relied on their discipline and decision-making throughout their lives. If you find putting aside your ego difficult, then prepare yourself to tap into patience you thought you never had.

By not taking personally what is said and done, Leaders engender a freedom of expression from which great ideas can emerge. When team members aren't stifled by the fear of offending or being criticized by a Leader, they unleash their creativity from which powerful ideas may spring forth. A Leader creates and sustains an expert team in the following ways:

1. Finding the right people
2. Constantly adapting to change

3. Acting as a coach and mentor
4. Getting your team to gel
5. Sending team members out to grow their expertise
6. Retaining team members
7. Building momentum
8. Maintaining momentum
9. Refining Leadership skills

1. Finding the Right People

Great teams don't happen by accident. Leaders are called upon to diligently prepare. They must have knowledge of what makes a great team. Leaders are responsible for deciding what mix of professionals they need, including specific skill sets. They must have a sense of the exact expertise required to achieve their purpose. Leaders will be held responsible for their team's results. This will be a measure of whether they appointed the individuals best suited for the job. Meeting high standards of excellence may require replacing team members or training and mentoring those who need additional support to fulfill their roles.

Before an expert team exists, it begins with a Leader's vision. A Leader's self-control, honesty, sincerity, integrity, transparency, and clear communication skills will be the model for all members added to an expert team. When Leaders fall short of upholding these qualities, they are sowing the seeds of mistrust and discord within the group. Once these poisonous seeds take root, they are a ferocious weed that can destroy whatever is in its path.

Leaders establish clear expectations and know each participant's role within the group. They understand each person's strengths, concerns, and hopes for the organization. An expert team is one where each member has a specific skill set that connects with the entire team. In fact, one key characteristic of expert teams is that they don't require the Leader to micromanage or be part of every step of the action plan.

It is through the Leader's careful selection process that individual accomplishment and drive result in group excellence. Contrast this with an inferior team: A leader demands to be at the center and participants to circle around him or her. This is often a sign of leadership cowardice, where he or she fears letting go of control and trusting others to fulfill their duties on their own. The consequence may be that team members feel they are not essential and not being recognized for the group's success. De-energizing the team always results in less satisfying outcomes.

Having an expert team is tremendously rewarding. Knowing your team can take on whatever task or project set before them provides peace of mind but typically requires a tremendous time investment. Every moment you invest supporting your team to perform at its best is energy well spent. Group productivity will be consistent and sustainable, and all participants will enjoy and find fulfillment in what they do. Over time, the group will work as one unit and perform to its fullest potential. A unified expert team is usually capable of more success than any individual can accomplish on his or her own. By collaborating, members combine their individual efforts and work as a group toward reaching a singular goal.

The collective force of a team is not the same as homogeneity. While an expert team is renowned for its accomplishments, collaboration, openness, goal orientation, and commitment, individual members possess different capacities in each area. In other words, within the collective are diverse participants with various ideas about the project at hand. The disadvantage of differing viewpoints is that conflict can arise. When mutual respect and striving toward a common goal serve as the foundation between team members, differing perspectives are encouraged and considered rather than inhibited and rejected.

A homogeneous team, one that comprises individuals with similar viewpoints, may work well together. But similar mindsets can lack the creativity required to solve big problems and innovate.

Once Leaders have designated individuals to fill roles within the team, they continually extend resources and time to help each person be the best possible participant. They consistently monitor each member to make sure his or her skill set and expertise match the position he or she occupies. Even the strongest leaders will experience only marginal success when they have placed the wrong person in the wrong position.

Bringing together a group of people who individually have stellar performance isn't enough. Building team integration is a lengthy process and a Leader's challenge. Team cohesion requires introducing specific opportunities and methods to the group. There are no shortcuts or easy formulas to create integrated groups that are committed, agile, and collaborative. Every Leader begins by using his or her experience and investing time to building trust among individuals. Once Leaders have done their part by providing opportunities and methods that give rise to integration, the team then is tasked to work toward it. Each team member's commitment to integration results in a culture of collaboration within departments and the organization itself.

2. Constantly Adapting to Change

Successful organizations are masters at adapting to change. Netflix launched a breakthrough business of mail order DVDs that accelerated the demise of brick-and-mortar movie rental stores. When DVDs became obsolete, Netflix evolved. The company not only entered the online streaming business but also created original video content. Suddenly, a company that seemed going the way of Blockbuster Video began taking away market share from the Hollywood studio establishment. A company that had multiple near-death experiences made a dramatic and surprise move by competing against a massive and powerful industry that seemed invincible. In short order, it became a foremost producer of original content.[1]

Had it not been for the company's CEO, Reed Hastings, and an expert team behind him, Netflix would have never survived the multiple

1 Siddhant Jain, "History of Netflix—Founding, Model, Timeline, Milestones (2024 Updated)," VdoCipher, July 21, 2024, https://www.vdocipher.com/blog/2017/06/netflix-revolution-part-1-history/#3.

life-threatening attacks against it. Hastings had a vision to not only keep his company afloat but also move it in a high-risk, new direction that had the potential for big payouts. His company's success was made possible by an expert team that executed his vision and evolved right alongside him.

Leaders like this have a time-traveling quality to them. These gifted men and women have a keen eye on the future and an understanding of consumer need that outflanks their competitors. Reflecting on the astonishing achievements of these exceptional individuals, we're left wondering whether they have special insight that gives them the ability to make bold, dramatic decisions that produce remarkable, sometimes history-making, results. Their vision is rare, and their skill at articulating and planning for innovations that move their industries quantum leaps forward make them legends. While their individual accomplishments bring them fame within their respective domains, time travelers such as Jeff Bezos, Richard Branson, Elon Musk, and Reed Hastings have reached innovative heights through fully integrated teams that bring their visions to fruition.

Leaders are team recruiters. But their role goes beyond filling spots with professionals. They continually fine-tune. Imagine a team is assembled that is responsible to start a new entrepreneurial venture within the larger organization. The Leader finds individuals with startup experience. They have vision, enthusiasm, and a spirit that inspires others outside the team and within the broader organization to believe in the new endeavor and participate in its execution.

As time passes and the organization continues to expand, it will need professionals who have skills ready to meet the demands of successful growth. Leaders are responsible to determine which skill sets are no longer needed or obsolete. In that case, the challenge is to provide employees the support and training necessary to develop new skills to learn, evolve, and remain productive. Those that are highly motivated to grow can be a great boon—their history and knowledge of the organization merged with new abilities is a powerful combination. If, however, change is too much for them, Leaders are tasked to make difficult and painful calls.

Leaders benefit from creating a culture where all team members are expected to grow and remain relevant. Employees may have joined an organization during its beginnings. As the organization evolves, new skills have been required to address expansion, product development, marketing and public relations, advanced technology, government regulation, contract negotiation, and multiple areas that are more crucial now than they were previously. If the organization's culture of continual improvement and evolution is embedded within it, then employees unable to meet this standard may understand they are no longer needed. As a result, they may self-select out of their current position or the organization itself. In order to transition to another organization that fits them better, they may require additional support.

When Leaders ensure their teams evolve alongside their organizations, they are better able to assess the credibility of opinions within their teams. Dissenting voices, rather than irrelevant and obsolete, may hold the key to the next great success. Leaders benefit from developing processes designed to improve intra-team communication and action. Once consensus is reached, everyone should align his or her efforts toward a common objective.

As an organization's needs and direction change, the team must be in favor of this movement forward. In addition, a Leader is responsible to adjust the team's composition in order to meet new and ambitious objectives and the obstacles that will emerge.

3. Acting as a Coach and Mentor

Leaders know their teams well. From the start of building their teams, they realized what expertise they needed to reach their ambitious goals. In other words, they searched for the right people to fill the right spots. Leaders know their team members' strengths and weaknesses. Part of a team's success comes from the collective expertise built upon individual gifts and talents. Thus, no one team member excels in every aspect that a team needs to succeed.

A Leader determines the area in which each team member needs help and then provides the resources to address and improve areas of difficulty. This may be through direct one-on-one coaching or steering the individual toward a solution.

Each team member is in a different place in his or her career. By virtue of your role as a positional Leader, you have more information and experience than those on your team. You probably also have more passion than the group you're spearheading. Thus, they do not know what you know. They may not have the fervor for the group's mission that you do, and they may not even want it—at least at the onset. Allowing others' capabilities—or lack thereof—to unfold as they develop their skills requires tremendous patience.

For people to grow professionally, they need the self-awareness to identify their strengths and weaknesses. From this point of understanding, they can determine what they need to learn and the resources they require in order to best contribute to the team. Then there are those who lack this self-awareness. This may be a result of fear, lack of trust in themselves and others, unpleasant past experiences, or apathy. There are innumerable silent and complex barriers.

Helping team members figure how to improve their professional performance requires scheduling time for discussion. It is essential to show respect for their expertise and to structure activities so each member feels included. The Leader's goal is to provide team members opportunities to share. This requires a high level of consistent patience on the part of the Leader. It is likely this time together will prove to be mutually beneficial. Think of this as an opportunity to incubate new ideas and listen firsthand to what it feels and looks like functioning in the space where the team member lives.

As all Leaders have learned throughout their careers, even their best idea will die if it is not expressed clearly and in a way that engages stakeholders to consider it. Team members frequently require guidance on ways to improve how they express themselves. Effective communication is an art and one that requires specific techniques and regular practice. Sometimes team members need guidance on how to improve their presentation skills. This includes the proper way to prepare ahead of time before pitching a plan they're passionate about.

Some team members have personal weaknesses that impede their ability to communicate great ideas to others. Consequently, they may struggle to deepen their professional connection with their colleagues. A lack of communication skills may prove to be an obstacle in their ability to reach their fullest potential within the organization.

Imagine a team member we'll call Mark. He is respected for his hard work and discipline. But he also has earned an infamous reputation as being defensive. When a colleague questions Mark on a point he's made or a decision he's considering, he interprets this as a personal attack on his intelligence and character. His sometimes-abrasive reactions cause his colleagues to view him as narrow-minded, unfriendly, and even unapproachable. They know if they say something Mark disagrees with, they may be treated harshly.

The team's Leader realizes Mark's area of weakness is minor relative to his strengths that contribute to the team. In addition, once Mark overcomes his defensive tendency, he will be an even greater asset to the organization. His team Leader should provide Mark with an objective perspective that brings awareness to his shortcoming and strategies that can result in his self-improvement.

Building expert teams requires that Leaders support others. A Leader has foremost training, experience, and knowledge. Providing these to team members is one effective way for a Leader to fulfill his or her commitment to team excellence. If done well, team members will grow right alongside you as you work together toward meeting your common objective. Mutual growth and a commitment to continually focus on it are how Leaders realize their most ambitious goals.

4. Getting Your Team to Gel

Imagine you're attending a meeting with your team. They've been relentlessly working toward a goal. You've been part of this plan, but you've also been busy running your organization.

During a group discussion, a team member makes a powerful point. The rest of the team members identify this spark of insight and respond using the same words. It may be "You hit it!" or "Boom!" or simply "Yes!" or any other phrase they share. Whatever it is, you realize they've used it among one another frequently enough to where they all say it in a mutually understood way.

This example is one of many that demonstrates when a team has gelled. Gelling takes many forms, and as in this case, it shows how the team has created its own language and culture. For Leaders, this is a proud moment, highlighting that one significant mission has been accomplished: They have created a cohesive team persevering toward goal accomplishment.

Gelling is not the same as groupthink. It is not a religious, cultlike, unchallenged allegiance to a particular dogma. Rather, gelling comes from vigorously presenting and evaluating various options. Once ideas have been proposed and arguments have been presented, a particular decision is made, and the team moves forward in this agreed-upon direction. Rather than discouraging dissent, gelling encourages it when done in a logical, reasonable, and respectful way. Gelling combined with a strategic plan produces powerful results.

Team members have different skills and approaches; they direct these toward a unified objective. When obstacles arise, which is to be expected when moving beyond chicken goals, gelling pushes a team to develop solutions to complex problems.

No team ever gels without an element of trust. This faith in others manifests itself in different ways, depending on the context. The varying degrees of trust are as diverse as the people who form teams.

Some people naturally exude an open attitude that inspires trust. Other people may be harder to know, and still others may consistently struggle earning one's faith and confidence. Reaching a point where a group shares a circle of trust is the endgame for any Leader responsible for his or her team's productivity.

Leaders cannot demand or require trust. It is a human dynamic that flourishes in some organizational cultures and yet does not remotely see the light of day in others. What is the difference between a team that learns to trust each member and one that continually engages in backbiting, one-upmanship, or silo behavior?

The responsibility resides with the Leaders themselves. To begin, they must be a model for trust. If they've had the privilege of bringing their team together, then their responsibility is even greater. Leaders who walk into a previously established team undoubtedly face challenges when it comes to earning trust. They must deal with people they did not select and a history that predated their involvement. Whether cultivating trust is relatively easy or extraordinarily difficult, it is a prerequisite for building expert teams. A high level of trust shared within a team is necessary for its success and ability to reach goals.

5. Sending Team Members Out to Grow Their Expertise

To include a person on a team, Leaders have taken great care assessing their organization's needs and vetting candidates. Leaders encourage, reward, and cultivate their team members to develop more expertise, not less. The more team members deepen their knowledge and skills, the greater contributions they'll make to the team. By growing their expertise, team members continue to engage themselves with their work and play a role in the culture of perpetual growth for the entire team.

Leaders are charged to expose team members to diverse perspectives and approaches that inform their work. Imagine a company is researching storage facilities. Its team members are tasked to see how other companies address their storage needs. The company may look at hospital settings, hotel venues, cruise ships, and other businesses challenged by a lack of space. Exploring organizations beyond one's own sector can often provide fresh, valuable perspectives. New ideas undoubtedly inspire decisions.

Sometimes employees of one organization are presented with the opportunity to work closely with another organization. These employees and their teams should be provided with clear expectations regarding what they will accomplish during their time away from their daily work. Working for a short time in another environment is an extraordinary opportunity for professional development. It is worthy of praise and appreciation from a person's employer. Not only does team members' time away expand horizons; it also allows them to better evaluate the processes and systems they use in their own work. In the short- and long-term, employees, their employers, and the other company benefit from this collaboration, comingling of ideas, and sharing of time and talent.

Prohibiting employees from working with other organizations is narrow-minded and archaic. Jealously guarding their skills and talents neglects to consider the benefit the employee will receive by building upon his or her mastery through hands-on work. The likely outcome is the employee will be more engaged and motivated by his or her work.

Leaders can also introduce teams to provocative thinking that exists within the organization or affiliated groups that support their industry. Conferences and workshops are the most common opportunities for professional development. Higher-level teams have more than likely experienced many opportunities for these standardized experiences.

Beyond conferences and workshops, growth and development may take different approaches. Encouraging team members to regularly attend civic or professional organizational meetings can help them learn about their communities. Chambers of Commerce, Rotary International, and Kiwanis clubs are examples of service organizations that team members may benefit from being a part of.

High-level team members are often requested as participants in feedback forums, focus groups, accreditation or certification groups, or even statewide problem-solving committees. Participation in diverse professional organizations expose team members to individuals operating within a wide range of professional environments.

It is not enough for Leaders to encourage team members to participate in these professional growth and development opportunities. Debriefing and following up with team members afterward is an important next step. When Leaders take time for these employees to share their observations from such outside professional experiences, Leaders increase the likelihood team members will apply their insights to their current assignment.

6. Retaining Team Members

When Leaders create expert teams, they always risk becoming victims of their success. Great teams are made up of exceptional individuals, and these ambitious men and women often become the focus of other leaders who want them on their teams.

You have pushed your team members to tap into their potential. They've relentlessly strived for excellence. What better employee have you prepared for your competition? Poaching top talent is a common practice among competing organizations.

While you've built a strong professional family and you know they are capable of gelling over the long term, you must also always realize that individual members may leave. Your hope is that when they depart, they do so with a positive impression about your organization. Sometimes you'll be the one responsible for letting a team member go. Your organization's needs have changed, and as a result, you may no longer have a place for them. While losing people may not be the worst hit your organization takes, you hope their departure doesn't strengthen the competition.

A conscious effort to retain talented staff requires a careful balance. It is vital that employees at every level are given clear expectations. The purpose of an organization's work, which in large part is what employees perform, can be their greatest motivation.

Studies have shown that a commitment to purpose often far outweighs issues related to compensation and benefits. Generally, purpose is articulated in the mission and vision, but real organizational purpose assures that the mission and vision are embodied in the company's working values. Purpose must be manifested in an obvious way in the day-in and day-out work everyone does.

Within my organization, for example, our core competency is transforming lives of at-risk students. For us, they come first. If you spend time in our offices, you'll see our staff working diligently to uphold this core competency. It manifests itself in the small and big tasks employees complete every day.

A school that claims to put students first would have this value clearly articulated in the school's vision, mission, and basic values. But beyond words, the value must be embodied in the daily work, processes, systems, and conversations of everyone involved. Unfortunately, it's far too common for organizations to give lip service to their purpose. They may state one thing and in fact live their professional lives in an entirely different way. This misrepresentation is disingenuous. It will more than likely result in the inconsistency between what's said and what's done.

Whether the organization is big or small, a workplace that provides psychological and physical safety is essential to retaining team members. A psychologically safe workplace does not allow bullying and discourages one-upmanship.

When done right, workplace competition can inspire and motivate people to perform at their best. Bullying and one-upmanship, however, are negative manifestations of competition. Here, backstabbing, betrayal, and secrets are the means to power. This hostile setting leads to burnout where people flee the negative workplace. A psychologically safe, professional environment is where people are encouraged to share ideas and work freely. Team members feel nurtured and valued.

A sense of psychological safety is greatly dependent on an individual's maturity, both personal and professional. There are times when ideas are shared or requests are made and the response is simply no. A generation accustomed since a young age to instant gratification and endless affirmation may struggle with adjusting to the workplace at odds with such an obliging background.

Not all ideas or suggestions can be accepted all the time. There are many reasons why what someone proposes is rejected. In the best scenario, this individual will receive the reasons behind a no, which include challenges or constraints. The person may be told that while the idea is good, the timing is not. Often, however, explanations may not be readily available. The employee may not be privy to all the reasons behind a no. The immature and inexperienced employee takes a no as a personal attack or rejection. Meanwhile, the mature and experienced employee understands the rejection may be the result of multiple logical factors that have little to do with the proposal itself. The bottom line is a no doesn't necessarily represent a toxic, mean-spirited, insensitive, unaccommodating, or inflexible workplace.

A physically safe workplace goes beyond those workplace protocols required by law. All employees must have a sense of physical safety and comfort that enables them to work efficiently. Boxes stacked on the floor, piles of files on tables, and dead plants are safety hazards and decrease efficiency. Leaders are responsible to think hard about how to create safe, efficient work environments for their employees. This includes how quickly their employees can access the materials they need to perform their jobs well, the space in which they work, and how their physical needs are addressed. Access to restrooms, water, kitchens, and efficient air circulation are aspects of physical safety.

Within our organization, we believe that clutter—toys at the desk, excessive Post-its framing monitors, notes dotting walls, and more—create mental distractions and slow creativity. Clean, open spaces are more efficient, and this applies to big spaces such offices and cubicles, as well as small ones such as desks, drawers, and bookshelves.

If team members prefer to work with music in the background, they use earphones rather than music playing through speakers that distract others. For Leaders and team members alike, it's easy to become immune to the minute details that can demonstrate either an inefficient, unsafe workspace or a safe, productive one. This is not to say thousands of dollars must be spent in creating luxurious offices or work areas. Cleanliness and a lack of clutter enhance any setting. What is important is that thought, creativity, and consideration be given to where people work, how they access the materials they need, and how their physical needs are addressed.

Last and most important is the ongoing opportunity to gain mastery, which allows employees to grow professionally. Most team members at every level highly value the chance to improve at the work they do. Supplying an overabundance of tools to accomplish that work isn't enough. Training and experience that improve mastery are necessary to support the engagement of employees at every level. These are the basics to retaining great staff who learn over the course of the many years that they may continue to work within the organization.

All employees are an investment, and from the time they're hired, the organization is responsible to see that this investment is fostered and nurtured for the long term. The balance comes into play when a Leader inadvertently communicates that an organization could simply not exist without that employee. It should be clear to the Leader and everyone in the organization that each person is replaceable, including the Leader. The balance then is in the understanding that there is a reciprocal relationship between the Leader and the team member. The organization benefits from the employee's work, and the employee benefits from being part of a professional, high-functioning, and caring organization.

7. Building Momentum

From articles and podcasts to everyday conversations, we constantly read and hear the words *change* and *innovation*. We associate both with a better life, which is a top priority for countries throughout the modern world. Central to this mission is technology that has increased lifespans, decreased infant mortality, made communities safer, provided new means of entertainment, and introduced countless other benefits. Whether Leaders are thinking on a grand scale, such as educating thousands of at-risk students, or on a personal level, such as improving their own lives, creating momentum that results in tangible and beneficial outcomes is the challenge.

Why is it, then, that Leaders concentrate on the concept of change without deeply considering momentum, which is necessary to create lasting, high-impact improvements within any organization?

No significant change occurs unless we apply some force or energy to it. For example, you may seek to work on an advanced degree or purchase a home. Initial steps include researching and completing an application. Without taking these preliminary measures, your objective never moves beyond your imagination. To turn a goal into reality requires taking a series of actions that builds momentum and takes you to your desired destination.

Momentum requires time, energy, avoiding what will hold you back, and focusing on what will propel you forward. But most importantly, Leaders must possess concentrated commitment that results in developing a rhythm and energy that will lead them to their goal.

Laozi, the ancient Chinese philosopher, said, "The journey of a thousand miles begins with a single step." Every day, Leaders work to inspire progress and change around them, including within their teams. Taking the critical first step is essential to developing the force necessary to show progress. With our busy lives that will only grow more intense with rapid and unrelenting technological advances, maintaining the laser-sharp focus necessary to advance toward consequential and meaningful goals will become more difficult over time. Staying on track to cross the finish line requires expert organization, time management, and discipline.

Leaders are typically rewarded for their skillful allocation of resources and time and their wise planning through signs they are headed in the right direction. These include observable change that can be measured both qualitatively and quantitatively. Those who are on the same journey and have special interest in the outcome your organization seeks may provide affirmations.

Hearing statements such as "I'm working on something similar. That's an interesting approach I haven't thought of" from trusted and credible sources is valuable information. Or affirmations may come from those who aren't involved in your work but will benefit from your products or services. These people have a direct interest in a positive outcome of a plan you have in place, and this may motivate them to express their opinions.

Often a team's greatest obstacle to building momentum is its fear of the unknown. Leaders may struggle, thinking that their team members are lazy and not open to moving forward. In many instances, idleness is a result of not knowing how to begin progressing toward one's goal. Or it can be due to procrastination from information overload.

In addition, team members may bristle thinking about uncertain outcomes. But upon further examination, any limitations, obstacles, and constraints may be more imagined than real. This means overcoming them may require nothing more than ignoring self-limiting beliefs and taking a single step forward.

From the individual to the group, working within an organization that fosters and nurtures how to tackle the unknown in a reasonable and productive way is a privilege. Momentum builds more efficiently when we set a goal and apply the energy, time, and resources to achieve it.

When Leaders train and support their teams in the practices that build energy, including instilling in them productive ways of living and working, momentum increases in scale. The impetus a team creates working toward a common goal builds upon itself. Successful businesses around the world have attained their place at the top by collective action. Positive change does not happen by chance. It requires a conscious effort to improve productivity by directing a flow of unwavering drive that leads an organization toward its goals.

8. Maintaining Momentum

Once you experience positive outcomes, you have initiated the flow stage. If done well, the momentum you've built will be sustained, like a river's mighty current, by your team. In this way, momentum seems to take on a life of its own. The reality, however, is that your team members' contributions are feeding this flow.

A high degree of momentum can be maintained only when an organization's culture is focused on positive disruption and radical innovation. Such a culture encourages and rewards individuals to carry an ambitious plan forward. Keeping consistent motion requires striking the balance between steadfastly working toward a goal and adapting to change to overcome inevitable obstacles that arise.

Once momentum is built, without a motivated team, it will fade out and eventually die. Organizations execute plans using momentum. But beyond these individual plans, this forward-moving urge must drive the entire organization itself. It is the life force necessary to grow and thrive when adversity and relentless pressures of outside influences strike.

There are four ways to maintain momentum. First, keep improvement incremental. Every manager or leader is expected to continually strengthen the organization. Sustainable survival requires constant energy placed on a process-oriented and systematic improvement. Encourage employees every day and reward them at least annually for taking action that benefits the organization.

Second, use adjacent innovation. Take advantage of what is already successful within your team and expand that process. For example, many organizations can duplicate their achievements using their existing technology or other resources.

Third, use disruption as motivation. Innovation is often met with opposition from others within and beyond your sector. When you're radically improving your industry, naysayers will criticize you. This is often a sign to keep pushing ahead.

Fourth, make it radical. When you create a breakthrough product or service that solves a major problem through taking a new approach, your desire to spread your discovery and improve as many lives as possible will motivate you.

Not all leaders are interested or prepared to build and maintain the momentum necessary to introduce sweeping new paradigms that will be sought-after and a template for widespread adoption. Unfortunately, neglecting to embrace the principles of building and maintaining momentum has consequences for your organization. Examples include risking being overtaken by competitors. Or your team may be ill-equipped to course correct effectively, which requires the capacity to take swift and prompt action to maintain operations and provide products or services. On the other hand, those organizations that embrace and pursue the principles of momentum are prepared to withstand and thrive against the constant and growing headwinds that today's organizations face.

9. Refining Leadership Skills

When it comes to professional development, teams can be taken only as far as Leaders have gone in their expert journeys. If Leaders have stopped working on improving their own skills, they are limiting the potential growth of their team members. Thus, Leaders must focus on honing their expertise from the moment they've envisioned themselves as a Leader to their very last breath; continually working toward being the best version of themselves becomes a lifelong practice that never stops. They identify what characterizes a happy, productive life and are passionate about continual improvement. This requires contemplation and reflection. Rather than an arduous chore that must be completed, refining Leadership skills can be energizing and a fulfilling part of one's daily life.

Leaders continually refine calmness, humility, generosity, spirituality, and the ability to visualize. Mastering these qualities gives rise to the hallmarks of Leadership—immense creativity and remarkable problem-solving. Leaders have a dream and then create a practical and substantive application for it. The creativity they develop influences how they understand the world around them and the role they play in it. Whether or not Leaders had confidence and courage from the start, groundbreaking accomplishments and successful innovations breed boldness unique to the Leadership journey.

What motivates a person to develop and then achieve greatness is partially a mystery. A Leader's understanding of power and how to use it constructively makes Leaders exceptional. If a Leader's version of power were readily accessible, then anyone with a desire for it could attain it. If a Leader's motivation were completely understood, it could be easily duplicatable. In fact, innumerable individuals aspire and work toward this kind of power, but most fail. Power demonstrated by Leaders has an elusive aspect. At the same time, study, discipline, sacrifice, and stepping back and freeing your team to work to its potential are concrete characteristics that all powerful Leaders have.

Summary

Although history recognizes individuals for their achievements, whether they be entrepreneurial, military, sociopolitical, scientific, or so on, only through teamwork do Leaders accomplish goals worthy of their legacy. A Leader's ability to succeed is directly connected to the quality of his or her team. The accomplishments or failures of an organization rest largely on its teams, whose performance is a direct reflection of its leaders. Thus, skillfully building teams is a Leadership requirement and a measure of a Leader's prowess.

Assembling individuals with different strengths, weaknesses, and personalities and having them work as a team to achieve greatness on behalf of their organization are tremendous challenges for Leaders. These are also among the biggest feats they can accomplish in their careers.

In the next chapter, you'll learn the seven qualities that set Leaders apart and that they continuously work to perfect.

Chapter 9

ESSENTIAL LEADERSHIP QUALITIES

When a thoughtless or unkind word is spoken, best tune out. Reacting in anger or annoyance will not advance one's ability to persuade.

—**RUTH BADER GINSBURG**, US Supreme Court Justice

BY 2008, STARBUCKS had expanded from its modest Seattle roots to become a household name around the world. The company had upgraded an otherwise humble and basic beverage for most American coffee drinkers into an artisanal experience to be enjoyed in its beautiful and bustling stores. Starbucks dotted airports, malls, and drive-throughs and became the go-to place for customers to read books, socialize, and network. To create an atmosphere of exclusivity, employees are commonly referred to as baristas, beverage sizes are labeled in Italian, and stores are comfortable places to relax and listen to its background music playlists that became popular and available for purchase.[1]

Beyond the United States, Starbucks had become a global brand with voracious expansion ambitions. At the same time, the company's aggressive growth coincided with a period of economic turmoil throughout the world. The Great Recession caused consumers to cut spending. Meanwhile, McDonald's and Dunkin' had created rival and lower-cost products that took away Starbucks's market share. Sales plummeted and stores were forced to close.

The company responded to the downturn by replacing its CEO with Howard Schultz. The famed founding father of Starbucks had stepped down as its head in 2000. He was now appointed to lift the company from its present troubles. As part of his turnaround plan, he assessed what had gone wrong. One of the problems he identified was the company's efforts to compete with fast-food chains. By doing so, it had diverted focus from its core product: coffee.[2] For instance, to attract customers who wanted a warm breakfast, the company had introduced morning sandwiches. But to Schultz's disappointment, the smell of heated breakfast sandwiches interfered with its image of welcoming guests throughout the day with coffee aroma.[3] So the company changed the recipe of its breakfast sandwiches. Its ingredients would no longer overpower the brand's famous coffeehouse smell. Placing the company's focus on its flagship beverage, rather than food and other products, was Schultz's top priority.

In his book, *Onward: How Starbucks Fought for Its Life without Losing Its Soul*, Schultz says, "Without great coffee, we have no reason to exist."

During his intense brainstorming meetings in early 2008, Schultz

1 Howard Schultz, *Onward: How Starbucks Fought for Its Life without Losing Its Soul* (New York: Rodale Books, 2011).

2 Nathaniel Meyersohn, "3 Times Howard Schultz Saved Starbucks," CNNMoney, June 5, 2018, https://money.cnn.com/2018/06/05/news/companies/starbucks-howard-schultz-coffee/index.html.

3 Lisa Baertlein, "Starbucks Now Says Will Keep Breakfast Sandwiches," Reuters, July 25, 2008, https://www.reuters.com/article/starbucks-idUSN25381863200807 25/.

asked his team to consider all options that would immediately put high-quality coffee at the top of Starbucks's priorities.

"The only way to retrain everyone by March is to close our stores, all at once," his team told him.

On the one hand, a massive company and nationwide training event made sense: The day after, every Starbucks barista would have received the same instruction, and thus every Starbucks customer would benefit instantly from this nationwide improvement initiative. On the other hand, the company would lose millions in revenue that day, competitors would swoop in and lure away customers, and cynics—including the media—could declare this drastic move as marking the beginning of the end for the famous company that was now in decline.

Schultz considered the major downsides of the plan and decided that the pluses made the effort worthwhile.

In his book, he says, "One Tuesday afternoon in February 2008, Starbucks closed all of its US stores. A note posted on 7,100 locked doors explained the reason: '*We're taking time to perfect our espresso. Great espresso requires practice. That's why we're dedicating ourselves to honing our craft.*'"[4]

Throughout the United States, when 5:30 p.m. appeared on each Starbucks clock, stores closed while all baristas remained on the payroll. Once all customers had left, employees watched a video made at the company's Seattle headquarters with short notice. All stores received the DVD accompanied by a DVD player. In it, Schultz gave an unscripted presentation:

> It is not about the company or about the brand. It is not about anyone but you. You decide whether or not it is good enough, and you have my complete support and, most importantly, my faith and belief in you. Let's measure our actions by that perfect shot of espresso.[5]

Schultz's bold action made national news—and in a positive way, which gave Starbucks free press, which is the dream of every organization.

---

4 Schultz, *Onward*, 3.

5 Schultz, *Onward*, 6.

In the end, his six-million-dollar risk paid off. Just as Schultz had hoped, his bold, risky move provided a powerful return on his investment. Coffee quality went up, and customers showed their approval through their patronage.

Schultz is known around the globe for making a small Seattle coffeehouse into a worldwide brand. The great risks he took that resulted in extraordinary success demonstrate his wisdom and ability to perform under pressure. By exhibiting essential Leadership qualities you'll learn about in this chapter, you too will prepare yourself to rise to the many major challenges all Leaders face throughout their careers.

■ ■ ■

The Leadership journey is mostly made up of uneventful incremental steps. But like the one thousand pieces in a puzzle, these small experiences combine to form the bigger, ambitious picture.

The following six areas are essential elements containing those small pieces that contribute to a Leader's growth from an enthusiastic rookie to a mature, highly effective, memorable Leader:

Taking responsibility for others

Learning to prioritize and organize tasks

Mastering strong communication skills

Taking chances

Dealing with difficult employees

Finding peace within the madness

Taking Responsibility for Others

Positional Leaders, prior to assuming their prestigious posts, often imagine how they would do things differently and what staffing changes they would make if they were in charge.

They may say to themselves when reflecting upon a colleague, "Michael's totally lost. I'd tell him exactly what he needs to do to set him straight." Or "Barbara is dead weight. She just slows us down. We don't need her. I'd get rid of her in twenty-four hours."

The reality is, however, those in charge at the moment may have similar thoughts and observations but also have multiple constraints out of their control that prohibit them from taking immediate action. If solving a problem was as easy as identifying it and then quickly implementing a change, the current Leader would have probably done so already.

Taking responsibility is how positional Leaders guide their teams and teach them to appreciate the direction and outcome that must be accomplished. Team members aren't always automatically sold on the goal they're tasked to reach. This may be because they do not understand the importance of what they're asked to do. But even when they do understand, indifference is a common response. They may be idle, be apathetic, or lack energy—within the workplace as well as outside it. Or they may be enthusiastic and eager to help, but they don't clearly understand what is being asked of them.

Your team consists of diverse individuals, and you may not have been the one who hired them. But now that you're in charge, you're accountable for your team's outcomes. Being responsible for others requires great skill and insight and is never easy. The greatest benefit of taking responsibility for others is that you can delegate to those who will effectively complete the task. At the same time, you are developing and preparing all team members so that in short order they too will be capable of completing difficult and challenging assignments.

All team members have their own strengths, shortcomings, insecurities, dreams, hopes, and disappointments. Outside of work, their personal lives influence and affect their worldview and general attitude and behaviors.

No one is immune from life's problems. Our elderly parents become ill and require caretakers. Relationships with people we care deeply about are often stormy seas that drain our emotional energy. Those of us who are parents have children that rightfully require a tremendous amount of attention and concern. People's financial security can be unstable and a huge burden. Many individuals at some point in their lives are afflicted with a hapless malaise that places a pall on the satisfaction they derive from their daily lives. Too often, young adults growing into their full maturity find the dreams and aspirations they once held now remote or even lost to them forever. The bottom line is that not everyone around us is downtrodden, but we all have challenges not apparent to the people we work with every day.

Leaders would never propose that intrusion into people's personal lives, invasive comments or actions, or overstepping professional boundaries is even remotely acceptable. At the same time, Leaders realize they are team builders. To perform this responsibility well, they understand that work and the requirements surrounding it do not exist in isolation. Teams comprise people that Leaders can support so all members may reach their fullest potential. Or in the case of poorly skilled positional leaders, their role may result in their staff feeling unappreciated, unworthy, unfairly burdened (such as when they are tasked to perform trivial work), or even alienated from the team.

All Leaders seek the following three characteristics from their direct reports: emotional intelligence, toughness, and dependability.

Emotional intelligence refers to a team member's savvy. Individuals with this trait are collaborative, people oriented, prudent, and focused. In addition, Leaders want team members versed in what's expected of them. They go beyond knowing how to simply execute their daily work and can perform their responsibilities in a manner that motivates and inspires the people around them.

Toughness does not suggest abrasiveness, aggressiveness, or insensitivity. Rather, it describes people not easily shaken by conflict, controversy, or other constraints that may emerge as they work toward achieving their goals. Tough people are strong, confident, and tenacious enough to see a task to its end.

Leaders seek **dependability** in team members. In today's workplace, people stay in a position for approximately two to three years. Unlike in previous generations, rarely are employees nowadays attached to a company or organization for even ten years.

As a result of this tremendous mobility, employees are often just settling in, understanding their work, and gaining experience when they move on to other positions that attract them. Developing loyalty—commitment to an organization or corporate culture—takes time. Leaders must first demonstrate in themselves the qualities they seek in their teams. They can inspire and attract others only when they themselves are authentic, genuine, and open to considering different perspectives. Loyalty and trust are rare and highly desirable. Relationships built on them should be sought-after, fostered, and nurtured at every turn. They are the opposite of artificial and insincere. If Leaders desire emotionally intelligent, tough, and dependable teams, then the responsibility to create these rests in themselves.

In the end, the patience and time required to retain highly valued individuals is worth the effort. When a team is truly enthusiastic, supportive, collaborative, focused, and committed to completing the work in a high-performing and intense environment, others outside your organization will notice. An emotionally intelligent, tough, and dependable team is the height of a Leader's accomplishment.

Learning to Prioritize and Organize Tasks

Every day has twenty-four hours. As much as many Leaders would prefer otherwise, they are bound to this time constraint just like everyone else. "I don't have enough time to get everything done" is the predicament most Leaders find themselves in. They are charged to solve multiple problems every day and nearly every hour.

Time management is an exhaustively studied subject. Consultants earn millions teaching corporations how to be more effective and efficient. After collecting mountains of data, their exhaustive reports often suggest reorganizing, incorporating trainings, and moving offices, furniture, and personnel around. But effective time management begins at the top and extends down.

As a Leader, how you accomplish your work sets the precedent for how others in your organization will perform their tasks. If leaders do not respect timeliness and solid deadlines, neither will their teams. If leaders accept what constitutes a very rough draft as a final product, then that becomes the acceptable standard of all final products. When leaders make excuses for incomplete or shoddy work, then excuses are what they should expect to receive from their team members. If leaders present work that isn't followed up on and appears to be nothing but busywork, then team members cannot be expected to seriously consider any urgency when a leader gives them a task.

Individualization and personalization are key time-management characteristics. Within my organization, we understand that everyone is different. Thus, each person has unique needs and solutions to accomplish work in an outstanding way.

Mary's Approach to Organizing Tasks

First, I tackle big tasks (which include ones I do not look forward to completing) as quickly as I can. For instance, if I'm fortunate to know of an obstacle ahead of time—many come without prior notice—I attack whatever elements of it I'm able to first thing in the morning. That may be by way of a meeting of significant consequence, emailing an important document, or traveling to an inconvenient or distant location.

By taking on major tasks immediately, I'm able to approach the work that follows and is of less importance without the stress of mulling over what I'll have to do later. In addition, if I defer tasks that I can take care of right away, I run the risk of them growing bigger and more unwieldy during periods of procrastination.

Second, I value maintaining a flexible calendar and scheduling time for personal work. While inputting meetings as calendar events, consider also entering the time you estimate you'll need to complete work. This allows you to accomplish tasks required to be effective during your appointments.

Third, I also view my calendar from a weekly perspective. During the weekend, I review what needs to be accomplished in the coming workweek. I then plan accordingly, inputting detailed information about each calendar event. I see what meetings I'll participate in and identify the main objectives and outcomes, as well as who will be present at each one. I identify the type of meetings I'll attend; some are brief where information is quickly shared among participants, while others are long and require preparing materials for intense brainstorming and project planning.

Fourth, I consider my schedule from a monthly perspective. For example, I look at my calendar and see that, three weeks from now, I have a meeting where I'll make a major presentation. I'll now create a deadline when I would like the presentation to be finished—and that deadline is never right before the meeting. I'm not one who performs at her best finishing tasks without a moment to spare. In fact, organizing and developing what I'll present during a meeting requires time. My work continues when I sleep—I'll often wake up in the morning inspired, head straight to my computer, and dash off a document with a clear perspective, which I spent a significant time developing. Thus, this monthly calendaring strategy suits my personality and how I work best.

Each Leader performs best under different circumstances. Thus, Leaders benefit from determining the optimal conditions they work under and, whenever possible, duplicating that setting.

Time management is a process of continual improvement. Although technology dramatically improves how we get things done, it has brought on more tasks we are charged to accomplish. Managing time well requires clear and orderly thought. You must determine the tasks that should be completed first and then the time necessary to complete each one. Within each task, is it possible to cut down the time you'll need without compromising quality?

Delegating responsibilities is essential to managing your time. Whenever possible, passing a task to another person will free your time to focus and take on responsibilities of greater importance. *If someone other than you can complete a task effectively, then by all means, pass it along to that person.* One of the marks of a Leader is his or her delegation skill. While only a Leader can complete certain tasks, beyond these, team members should be assigned responsibility. This demonstrates both the strength of those within the team and a Leader's delegation skill.

While a particular project may originate from a Leader's office, passing it to other team members enables Leaders to effectively oversee their multiple responsibilities. The Leader may check in on an as-needed basis and approve or course correct if necessary.

Leaders who regularly say, "I'll take care of it," when someone else can complete a task can cause frustration for the leader as well as team members. First, for those team members that want more responsibility, the leader is both thwarting their ambitions and diminishing their desire to serve the organization. Team members may also interpret the leader's insistence as a lack of trust in them. Second, leaders who have this habit increase the likelihood of personal burnout. Being in charge is an enormous responsibility, and Leaders must identify what they'll do and what they'll delegate to others to manage their time effectively.

Initially, Leaders benefit from modeling how to accomplish tasks and how to evaluate the quality of their outcome. Modeling is a powerful practice for tasks that will repeat. With effective training, within a short time, team members will be able to take on a particular responsibility with minimal input from the Leader. When modeling is done well, Leaders demonstrate their ability to know where to focus their time and energy. They're rejecting the false belief of "it won't be done right unless I do it" and avoiding overextending themselves.

Insecurities and fears sometimes motivate leaders to say, "I'll take care of it." In this instance, they're often trying to assert their importance within the organization and perpetuating the aura of being the sole person with certain secrets. Another motive is a desire to be perceived as the smartest person in the organization who has the answers that, like a comic book superhero, will save the day.

Fanatically protecting their proprietary information may be a way leaders assert their importance within the organization and a source of personal pride. They may believe the secrets they hold are job-security insurance policies that keep them relevant and cherished. "I am the only one that knows how to do this, and my organization couldn't possibly survive without this vital knowledge I hold close to my chest" reflects the faulty thinking of someone with this mindset.

Beyond the mental burden of this perspective and the possibility of burnout, this also does not play well with team members. An integrated, collaborative culture is a key characteristic of successful teams. The foundation of this culture is trust and a sense of personal empowerment that team members need to be effective participants.

Team members may rightfully disdain a leader's effort to keep them in the shadows and make them irrelevant. They may perceive themselves as being treated as children, rivals, or even enemies. Keeping team members in the dark halts a team's ability to trust one another and thus creates silos. In the end, leaders may be perceived as weak and insecure, which is the opposite of what they intend.

The rapid pace of technological advances brings about time management challenges. On the one hand, advanced devices and software have the potential to speed up task completion. On the other hand, the learning curve can be steep, time consuming, and overwhelming. To complicate matters more, some advances may not be worth your time and energy to adopt. In addition, the time-management tools you depend on today will not be the same ones you'll use in the future. Remaining open-minded and adapting rapidly to change are key. When used effectively, these tools will increase your efficiency and effectiveness as a Leader.

Mastering Strong Communication Skills

When addressing a group, large or small, keep your message as simple as possible. Always show how it relates to a larger, more significant goal. Clearly express what your audience needs to know, which is the "why" relating to what you're asking and, most importantly, what they'll be held personally responsible for.

When participating in a meeting with your peers and working with your superior, common tendencies arise that interfere with productive meetings. One stems from a participant's need to be in the spotlight. In this scenario, a question is posited to the group. A person rushes with an answer to draw attention and impress others. As if racing in a sprint, this participant strives to come out early and fast with a reply to cross the finish line before anyone else. Most often such quick responses are not original. Thus, the facilitator, as well as the participants, has already heard a version of what this individual scrambled to say.

Don't be this person. Those in positions of authority want concrete, insightful, and relevant contributions that inspire additional discussion. Most often these do not appear in a participant's mind right away.

Being asked for your opinion is often a sign of the gravitas you hold in the group. Take the opportunity to express yourself seriously. A calm, confident description of your ideas carries much more weight than a rushed message expressed for the sake of being first. When you offer your superior perspective after all others have shared theirs, you have left a powerful impression on the group. More importantly, you are demonstrating how your contribution to the team will move it closer to reaching its goal.

When it comes to written communication, whether in print or electronic, make sure it always reflects the highest level of professionalism. Both intra-team communications and ones sent to contacts outside the organization should always be well written, be edited, and include a time stamp.

When it comes to verbal communication in large groups, as well as one-on-one settings, solid listening skills are essential. Maintaining objectivity and thoughtful nonverbal communication are the main characteristics of those who listen well.

In order to maintain objectivity, good listeners do not assume. They predict neither what the speaker will say next nor that they will understand what the speaker will tell them from the start. Oftentimes, a sign you're listening well is that you require more information or clarification from the speaker.

The downside of predicting what the other person will say is that it requires internal dialogue where you're thinking to yourself. You may be telling yourself how what you're hearing will or will not work and developing your response. This form of mental multitasking necessitates switching between listening to the speaker and listening to the comments in your head. In the end, you're not giving your full attention to either the speaker or your personal thoughts. You may wind up missing information significant to the organization or to a decision you must make.

Nonverbal communication is as real and as impactful as verbal communication. Thoughtful nonverbal communication means you realize how others perceive your body language, and you use it carefully. What you express through body language can influence what a speaker says to you. Nodding your head up and down says yes and side to side says no. Demonstrating your approval or disapproval this way may steer speakers into saying more or less and serve as a filter they use that keeps them from being forthcoming with their opinion. Developing your poker face will help you avoid influencing what the other person says to you and thinks you want to hear. At the same time, some people may struggle describing to you what's on their mind. In this instance, a subtle smile may set them at ease and motivate them to speak more freely.

If you want the person you're speaking with to express ideas candidly and honestly, then listen more and interrupt as little as possible. You may be speaking with someone who has more direct contact with a person or group within your organization than you have. He or she may not be as articulate as you but has valuable insights you wouldn't otherwise have access to.

Listening is part of communication, so how you hear what the other person says is just as important as what you say. Developing and upholding objectivity and thoughtful nonverbal communication does not happen on its own. Certainly, some people have better innate communication skills than others. But both groups benefit from focusing on continual improvement. Prior to each conversation, determine the outcome you wish to achieve, and during the discussion, maintain objectivity and thoughtful nonverbal communication. By doing so, you increase the likelihood that others will be honest and forthcoming with their opinions and observations and that all participants feel satisfied and respected.

Taking Chances

Some people are born risk-takers, while others take risks only when pressed. The degree of risk professionals must take within their organizations is one factor that separates Leaders from managers. Managers oversee and advance the status quo within their organizations. Doing so often actually requires mitigating or avoiding risk. They are generally not called upon to take large chances. While they may be required to implement a particular change, a positional leader has approved the change and assumed the risks associated with it.

Whether they relish risk or are averse to it, Leaders realize that taking chances is one of their responsibilities. They also understand that beyond risk-taking itself, decisions made must generate successful outcomes. Both their professional reputations and the organization's ability to advance in the marketplace require results that demonstrate worthwhile risk exposure.

In fact, Leaders have gained fame for their risk-taking that has vanquished competitors and elevated their organizations to dramatic heights. So-called turnaround Leaders enjoy taking chances to the point that they purposefully inject themselves into chaotic and failing organizations, intent on bringing order and prosperity to them. Even those that never plan to become experts in fixing broken companies will benefit from understanding the mindset of turnaround Leaders, as well as all who relish risk-taking and have had remarkable results.

Many times Leaders are thrown into difficult circumstances they didn't ask to be a part of and are tasked to solve problems they didn't create. But they've trained their entire careers to meet the demands placed before them. They understand the value of both the seemingly insignificant, small steps they must take and the big, audacious ones that will result in overcoming the adversity they face.

Like professional athletes, Leaders rely on a set routine that allows them to perform at a high level within tough environments. Part of a Leader's training to take on risk of increasing importance is accepting challenging professional assignments that present difficult problems to solve—often these are ones that others were unable to figure out. These assignments push Leaders to tap into their creativity in order to develop innovative solutions.

Taking on tough assignments is a tall order, and failure is always a possibility. But when confronted with a challenge, Leaders run toward it rather than away from it. A Leader's calculated and bold action, however, is not the same as reckless risk-taking.

Leaders leverage their wisdom to navigate through perilous professional waters. Here, as you've read in this chapter, they tap into the power of teamwork. For leaders to think they can solve a monumental problem on their own could be a sign of their delusions of grandeur. But when they are experts at building teams, they realize that tapping into the skills of talented, highly motivated individuals and the strength of effective teamwork enable them to wisely assume calculated risk with courage, grit, and confidence.

Taking chances to solve major problems or make significant improvements requires Leaders to focus their time and resources on an organization's strengths, rather than its weaknesses. Shifting a strength from ordinary to exceptional may be the key to elevating an organization to otherwise unattainable heights.

A business's strategic plan includes long- and short-term planning that centers on operational aspects that have been identified as critical for success. Where serious weaknesses in a process or system that helps run the organization exist, immediate action must be taken. A company hemorrhaging money must stop the bleeding. But barring such a severe problem, a thorough consideration of an organization's needs will likely uncover strengths within it. These offer hope for bigger and better achievements that overshadow any one problem.

In some instances, focusing on boosting current strengths may result in outcomes so positive and significant that weaknesses require less attention. A strength improved to a superb degree may be the toehold that lifts a project or the entire organization to a higher level of achievement and overshadows vulnerabilities.

In the case of your organization, rather than leave excellent aspects untouched for the sake of addressing weaknesses, consider how your business's strengths may be preserved and even parlayed into outstanding performance.

Within my organization, this was our strategy for continual improvement. Our team has adopted the word *stellar* to describe performance that we always strive to reach. Operating at this high level has often revealed the path to even greater success. In casual conversation within other organizations, attaining this degree of accomplishment is described as unlocking the secret, turning the key, or cracking the code. In the end, the secrets to success are not hidden at all. Our professional environment is rich in opportunities and options that can result in dramatic improvement.

Every day, we practice and train up-and-coming team members to identify a beneficial approach, further develop it, and deploy it throughout our organization. Once we've identified a successful function within our organization, rather than leave well enough alone, we do the opposite. We refine it until it reaches our definition of stellar. By building on our strengths and not just focusing on our weaknesses, we have brought about unparalleled high performance. As a measurement of our strategy's success, in 2015 and 2021, we earned the Malcolm Baldrige National Quality

Award, the nation's highest presidential honor for performance excellence through innovation, improvement, and visionary leadership. Our 2015 award was the first time it was presented to a K through 12 school—most importantly, a charter school—in the award's thirty-year history.

Dealing with Difficult Employees

In running your organization, you will inevitably encounter people who are angry. Isolated instances of such negativity can be readily tolerated. For some people, however, their relentless, extreme, and bitter attitude adversely affects those around them. Not exclusively due to issues related to the workplace, their anger may be rooted in a personal, deeply held rage that extends beyond the workplace but is initially attributed to it.

Troubled individuals almost have a quiet panic. They behave as a hurt, teary-eyed child, striking out in violent and unpredictable ways. They may reveal a stealth hysteria that drives them to take hurtful action against those they think have wronged them—a coworker, a colleague, a person of authority, or even a loved one. Frequent rants and clinging to minor issues are also characteristics of a bitter and self-defeating person no one really wants to be around, let alone work closely with.

I recall a young man who began his career at our organization and was well on his way to a series of lucrative leadership positions. He was hard-working, smart, and well-thought-of, and his supervisors were pleased to sing his praises. I'll never know for sure what caused a turnaround in his behavior, but I surmise that a bitter divorce, the loss of his home, and the stress associated with such upheavals taking place within a short time frame contributed mightily to it. After these adverse events, he became divisive, insincere, not generating trust, and undermining both leadership and colleagues—in other words, the opposite of who he had been when we hired him. His case is not exceptional. Many people throughout the country with bright futures have had their potential crushed by personal challenges they were unable to overcome.

Sometimes people's dark outlooks are hidden because they've mastered the ability to conduct themselves in a relatively civil manner. Their words and actions may in fact communicate great courtesy or even humility. But their negative side will eventually emerge. This often occurs when they face difficult circumstances.

People that take vindictive action do not always lose. They may succeed in their hurtful intention, and the leader or team or both suffer—at least in the short term. They wage war against anyone they feel has wronged them. But those with these extremely negative viewpoints will rarely consistently succeed, and it's guaranteed they have forfeited their long-term happiness. Meanwhile, their colleagues, team, bosses, and family members are subject to the dark cloud these angry people cast and the stress they spread to those around them.

Although a loved one or a coworker may use strategies to build trust or de-escalate this person's vexation, in many cases, those efforts are an exercise in futility. They do not placate and may even make a bad situation worse.

In the case of a work setting, Leaders determine whether they'll tolerate, address directly, or reject such behavior. The question of how to deal with an employee's disruptive conduct rests largely on the person's ability and willingness to choose to grow in a positive direction.

People can change for the better. Some may recognize the positive energy surrounding them and see their compulsively negative approach gets them nowhere. But as human behavior has taught us, such divisive people rarely voluntarily and dramatically change their perspective for the better. Most are committed to their way of thinking and refuse to improve. Unfortunately, individuals who have grown up in families that harbor hatred and anger are conditioned to perpetuate what they learned, and breaking these cycles often requires tremendous work.

In most instances, these troubled people use whatever imagined wrongdoing was done against them to justify their outrage and bad behavior. Over the years, wise colleagues and I have tried to discern how best to cope with these difficult people with whom we must work and require an inordinate amount of time and energy to deal with.

The strongest deterrent to an employee's anger or other negativity is to have a solid organizational culture that makes it obvious to the individual and everyone else around that such behavior is unwelcomed. Most often, these people will self-select out of a work environment where they do not feel accepted. In the meantime, leaders, managers, and coworkers must maintain calm and adapt whenever possible.

Frequently, the issue this irascible employee brings up is relatively minor and has an easy solution, which is not exceedingly hard for everyone else to live with. Sometimes placating this person is infinitely better than creating a major confrontation over some silly matter that has little impact on how the work is done or achieved.

But if a cooperative, conciliatory approach succeeds only in exacerbating this person's bad behavior, then at some point, Leaders must step in. When they do, they'll clarify specifically what the expectation and parameters are regarding this individual's interaction with coworkers and managers.

Aside from dealing with this professionally, I've also stepped back with sorrow and thought, "What a pity this person is expending so much energy motivated by hate-filled anger." These negative individuals are sometimes in their twenties, a period that should be the best times of their lives with a positive, enthusiastic future of opportunities and challenges.

In the case of working with people who fit this profile, either within or outside the organization, at times I've found envy is the basis for their disgruntled or moody demeanor. They often covet in others what they believe they don't have. This may be a person's position, power, or respect received, which inflames an unhappy person's sense of unfairness. They may be stuck in a mental loop of asking questions that trigger their outrage:

"Why shouldn't I be in the corner office surrounded by people doing my bidding?"

"Why do I lack loyal friends and colleagues?"

"Why am I not as well received as my colleagues?"

Meanwhile, it never occurs to these envious individuals that others may have gained their position or favorable place in life through sincere and collaborative hard work, which has earned them the admiration and confidence of those around them.

Who we are, what we are, and how we believe others perceive us form part of our most intimate thoughts. Most of us easily and naturally maintain the boundary between public and private disclosure of what's on our minds.

The default rule is to say less when one's uncertain about whether to express what one's thinking. Those with uncontrolled temperaments have an equally difficult time controlling what they say to others. Leaders responsible for a team are always challenged in these circumstances. They must endeavor to help all team members, including difficult employees, adjust to an open and collaborative organization. Leaders are charged to set boundaries. To what degree and lengths do they go in trying to support this person without being seemingly unjust to the coworkers suffering daily?

By applying the lessons in this book, you'll better understand and manage the more fragile members of humanity within your organization and network. But Leaders must regularly remind themselves that they too are susceptible to becoming one of these troubled people. Ongoing stress and strain can very easily result in the transformation of a once dynamic and passionate Leader into one of the burned-out has-beens, scattered along the roads of career paths gone awry.

Leaders at the highest level observe and know this lesson well. Throughout their career paths, they have taken time to appreciate the beauty and wonder that surrounds them. They have succeeded in drawing out the kindness, commitment, and dedication of others. They have remained whole by seeking solace, tranquility comfort, joy, and pleasure from their families and friends. Fun times, party times, quiet times, and deeply spiritual times come together to shape the resilience that every Leader must have to successfully live a long, productive career.

Finding Peace within the Madness

Every day, I have the pleasure of working with a group of individuals in my organization called the Leadership Team. They ensure the systems and ideas that professionals within our organization have created and have been approved are successfully implemented. In addition, the Leadership Team works to inspire innovation and change in others.

During our meetings, I regularly remind Leadership Team members to stay alert and open to the inspiration all around them. Seeking inspiration is a habit that, through consistent practice, can be mastered like any other. Because all members of the Leadership Team lead high-energy, vibrant lives filled with countless and large goals to accomplish, we must not lose sight of the events that unfold before us that can easily otherwise go unnoticed. We need to be mindful of them so they can inspire and encourage us.

While being productive and completing tough tasks is fundamental to high achievement, so is stillness. Positive and profound insights come when we least expect them and when we are open and aware of our surroundings. Maintaining long-term enthusiasm and motivation in a demanding profession is difficult, and through revelations—small and big—we see new possibilities that allow us to transcend our ordinary lives and limitations.

When we continually tell ourselves that inspiration is everywhere, we will find it—whether in the seemingly mundane (taking a walk, listening to music, or watching TV) or the profound (seeking a mentor's advice or experiencing an intense, unforgettable event).

In my home, I have a wall with notes I frequently look at. On it I post phrases that remind me to stay observant of my surroundings throughout the day. If I'm in need of inspiration, I know where to find it. Some of my favorite sayings are as follows:

> If you change the way you look at things, the things you look at change.

Raise your words, not your voice.

It is rain that grows flowers, not thunder.

Never give up.

Success breeds success.

When seeking inspiration, I remind my Leadership Team that doing so is simple but not easy: Make purposeful time for doing nothing other than to contemplate. This means scheduling moments to experience calm, quiet time alone. Examples include relaxing at the beach, sitting in the garden, hiking, or sipping a favorite cup of tea without engaging in other activities. All truly happy people take an occasional break from the hectic world to steep themselves in surroundings that bring them peace of mind, gratitude, joy, and creativity. By planning times of quiet contemplation regularly, you become a gift to your colleagues, your family, and most importantly, to yourself.

■ ■ ■

From professional athletes who had nervous breakdowns to executives who became drug addicts, stories of admired, accomplished people whose careers collapsed after cracking under pressure are familiar to us all. Sometimes they fail alone. Other times, they drag down those around them during their descent. They may blame their failure on others and even seek revenge as a means of compensation for how they were wronged.

Given the unrelenting strains of Leadership, finding peace throughout your professional journey is essential to long-term achievement. Although terminating employees, enforcing rules when they're broken, and dealing with innumerable other difficult circumstances can test your emotional stability, Leaders take such strong action with calm poise and do not succumb to angry, erratic, abusive behavior. Beyond this, they also are responsible to create a culture of joy during good times and bad that comes from within and spreads throughout the organization.

While countless reasons can account for failure, if it's the consequence of the pressures of high achievement, then finding peace within the madness is the remedy. Sustaining a high locus of control is key to maintaining peace despite the surrounding chaos.

When Leaders recognize that a calm state of mind comes from within rather than from external circumstances, they focus on what they can control and pay less attention to what they can't. They develop habits that increase serenity. Similar to how consistent exercise improves one's physical health, regular moments of reflection and contemplation improve one's mindset. These practices are performed both in the short and longer phases of our careers.

Taking brief walks throughout the week, having lunch quietly without smartphones or TV, participating in positive workplace conversations whenever possible, and taking a deep breath or counting to ten when triggered by stressful events are small, simple steps that, when done consistently, contribute to mental clarity. Regular vacations are longer-term practices that add to one's well-being. Also, adopting more formal habits of meditation will support Leaders' efforts to develop a self-image realistically projecting a reasonable, serene persona that gives confidence to people around them.

When Leaders can consistently find peace within the madness, they prepare themselves to deal with challenges without panicking, acting impulsively, overreacting, or succumbing to paranoia. By recognizing they are in charge and responsible for the outcome of any decision they make, they reduce the likelihood of making careless decisions. Being a Leader is a badge of honor. Leaders increase their ability to uphold the status of their position by enjoying regular moments of serenity and contemplation.

Summary

In this chapter, you've learned essential skills necessary to transition from emerging to fully formed Leader.

Leaders are respected and admired. At the same time, the essential elements presented in this chapter separate Leaders from those who aspire to but never take the leap. Or if they do try, they fall short of their hopes or expectations.

As this chapter has described, Leadership is a skill that is accessible to those who are called to it. By mastering what you've learned here, you're following a formula that, like a precisely aimed projectile pulled far back in a slingshot and released, will allow you to reach your professional target.

Your fellow Leaders are working tirelessly to improve their skills and stay at the top of their positions within their industries. This is why those who have occupied their roles for decades never stop reading and studying about their craft and identifying breakthrough research and trends. To stay relevant, you should too. With an unlimited number of books, articles, videos, podcasts, and blogs, today's Leaders have more resources than ever to maintain momentum and reach their highest professional potential.

In the next chapter, you'll learn the last stage of Leadership. Taking the quantum leap is embarking on a boundless journey marked with continual growth.

Chapter 10

A QUANTUM LEAP

FROM HIS DAYS at Harvard being a star student and athlete, Alan Bersin showed his exceptional ability to master different skills. As an undergraduate in 1967, he was considered one of toughest offensive guards in his college's history selected to the All-Ivy, All-New England, and All-East football teams. He was a member of the school senate and voted second class marshal. After graduating magna cum laude, he became a Rhodes Scholar, studying at Oxford's Balliol College. He then went on to earn his law degree at Yale in 1974.

From the East Coast, he went west and practiced law in California for seventeen years as a senior partner at Munger, Tolles & Olson. Afterward, President Bill Clinton appointed him chief federal law enforcement officer in the San Diego and Imperial Counties under the Department of Justice where he served for five years.

Bersin then took the leap from federal border czar to superintendent of San Diego City Schools, which is the nation's eighth-largest school district and second biggest in California. After seven years as superintendent, he was appointed the Golden State's secretary of education by Governor Arnold Schwarzenegger. A year later, Bersin was elected chairman of the San Diego County Regional Airport Authority, and three years afterward, he worked for the US Department of Homeland Security, then the US Customs and Border Protection, followed by INTERPOL. Later, he tapped into his executive leadership side when he became CEO of BorderWorks Advisors and executive chairman of Altana AI. He is a fellow at the Aspen Institute and Harvard's Belfer Center and a senior advisor at Covington & Burling LLP.[1]

Bersin is a rare Leader that has taken the **quantum leap**, which is high achievement in more than one sector. Examples of taking the quantum leap include excelling in two or more of the following: education, law, manufacturing, engineering, medicine, business, or public service. Once Leaders have gained skills and earned acclaim in one sector, rather than continue in the same one, those making the quantum leap break from their own status quo and move into another sector. They're often driven by a desire to apply their Leadership to improve and make a positive impact in a different industry. While continual accomplishment within one sector is an option, Leaders who make quantum leaps have always chosen challenges over comfort.

I had the privilege of working for Bersin during his tenure at San Diego City Schools. Since leaving that post, he has continued making quantum leaps with no slowing down in sight. Leaders like Bersin begin with a mix of intelligence, discipline, grit, commitment, and vision. From there they overcome an unending series of obstacles and constraints.

Len Hering is another example of a Leader that has taken the quantum leap. Since 2012, he has sat on CSSD's board. He started his career in the US Navy where he served for thirty-two years and earned the Navy Distinguished Service Medal and the Presidential Award for Leadership in Federal Energy Management in 2005. A career-long commitment to

1 Alan Bersin, Criminal Investigations and Network Analysis website, accessed November 29, 2024, https://cina.gmu.edu/people/alan-bersin/.

addressing national security, organizational efficiency, workforce development, sustainable behaviors, and the effects of climate change has informed all leadership roles he played in his wide-ranging military and civilian career posts. As a national board member of the Military Child Education Coalition, he helped address the challenges experienced by military children. After retiring from the navy, Len worked for the University of San Diego, was a founding member of the Plastic Ocean Project, and served as president and executive director of both the Center for Sustainable Energy and I Love A Clean San Diego. Today he is an active member of the Center for Climate Security and the American College of National Security Leaders and serves on a number of other boards. As former CSSD chairman of the board, he contributed to an open exchange of ideas that was most beneficial in solving many of the problems we faced.

The challenges all Leaders face—especially those aiming to take the quantum leap—crush most who aspire to leadership and lack the interest or fortitude to triumph over difficulty. Those who successfully do make the leap have charisma that attracts others to them. Even among detractors, many respect quantum-leap Leaders' determination and intellect. In this chapter, we'll explore the characteristics, habits, and mindset of Leaders who take the quantum leap.

Quantum Leaps and Legacy Leaders

To succeed, Leaders establish and accomplish goals of increasing importance that require taking on greater and greater responsibility. From there, Leaders delve deeply into the processes they need to reach their ambitious objectives. To execute their plans, they learn from others, address political constraints, and identify and then acquire resources required for goal attainment.

For Leaders to make a quantum leap, they must reach mastery over systems in different industries. Each sector they enter has its challenges and obstacles to overcome. Quantum Leap (QL) Leaders apply problem-solving talents and other diverse strategies that reflect their ability to adapt to change regardless of the sector.

These extraordinary men and women may make the leap by choice or by accident. Those who do so by choice may reach a point where they realize the skills they've honed and the knowledge they've gained have an application outside the industry where they've established their legacy. They come to understand leadership and organizational theory in a way that broadly encompasses many sectors, places, and circumstances. The confidence that grows within them as they reach the highest leadership ranks may extend to the team with which they work.

In my organization, I believe our Leadership Team has, as a result of many years of training and working at different positions, developed an outstanding capacity to apply their expertise to a different industry. I could foresee our Leaders lifted from their familiar professional surroundings to a radically different work setting in need of a turnaround. The work of these passionate, creative, productive individuals could transform a moribund organization into a thriving one.

But some Leaders that have taken the quantum leap have been ushered into new positional opportunities by their peers. Leaders such as Alan Bersin, for example, may have been presented with an opportunity to apply their talents and skills to a sector they never considered.

Whether purposeful or accidental, QL Leaders have reached the highest level of Leadership. Like Yoda, they are masters whose influence transcends specific industries, their insight and accomplishments are legendary, and they are exceptional individuals. Once the quantum leap is taken, their accomplishments create momentum that results in reaching new career heights and places they likely had not anticipated.

Leadership is a journey that follows set stages. It begins with peer power and from there shifts to expert power, purposeful power, power by accomplishment, expert team building, and refinement of Leadership skills. Many may not aspire to go beyond these steps. When remarkable Leaders, who are among an already rarified group, do, they embark on new paths that may result in quantum leaps.

During the careers of QL Leaders, a series of challenging doors open, and they boldly and successfully walk through them. Their body of work is recognized as a long-term force for positive disruption and improving the lives of others. They are the Leadership elite who are respected; their viewpoints are sought-after. Their Leadership is also multilevel, which means they've excelled in different roles. Michael Jordan went from the heights of NBA stardom to minor league baseball, all while building his business empire that includes sportswear, professional sports team ownership, and namesake restaurants. His career path demonstrates the multiple levels of success that Quantum Leap Leaders achieve.

The Evolution of Leaders Who Make the Quantum Leap

Leaders that have made the quantum leap initially gained their expertise in a specific area of study or professional sector. Within that area, they have built teams, successfully led projects, amassed a network comprising dedicated people, and received accolades for their accomplishments.

Through their years of experience, Leaders have worked with professionals in accounting, law, real estate, construction, transportation, marketing, public relations, information technology, and human resources; with government agencies; and with collective bargaining units. One cannot successfully make the quantum leap without being familiar with what these professionals do and the problems they're charged to solve. Leaders will apply this knowledge to new industries. When entering a different organization, they use their extensive expertise to identify weaknesses and strengths within it. Given their wide breadth of knowledge and track record of accomplishments, they are often sought out to turn around failing organizations. Other times, they're hired to take successful business to the next level of achievement.

QL Leaders are prepared to break the status quo when they deem it necessary to improve an organization. They are masters at questioning the status quo if they've determined it's not working. Despite being a disruptive force of positive change, when necessary, they proceed with their radical work with calm. They have unflagging optimism that expects productive outcomes from their hard work. Rather than seeking safety, they realize that taking calculated risk is a prerequisite to creating lasting change. In this regard, they are accustomed to stepping out of their zones of comfort. In fact, they seek challenges to overcome because professional growth and expanding their experience are their lifelong pursuits.

Rather than simply apply a formula they successfully used in one industry and transfer it to another, they constantly adapt to change and seek opportunities to learn by reading books, meeting with those that can widen their understanding, and attending conferences, lectures, workshops, and trainings. Masters at efficiency, they know how to quickly find the best resources to support the quantum leaps they take.

Quantum Leaps and Powerbrokers

All exceptional Leaders use power wisely. One aspect of Leadership is applying power to create professional networks. Quantum Leap Leaders are master powerbrokers. They use their power to exert influence.

Leaders as powerbrokers are sought-after for their expertise across multiple industries. Their renown and track record of accomplishments precede them. Masterful Leaders are often asked for insight in terms of the work others are doing. Legislators may seek the QL Leader's insight into a specific issue. Community leaders who are sorting out competing viewpoints often seek the wisdom and perspective of the sage and objective Leader. Up-and-coming professionals and executives covet the time when they have the ear of these highly accomplished people. Armed with a QL Leader's wisdom, corporate heads, legislators, entrepreneurs, business leaders, aspiring managers, and ambitious students are more likely to have a strong impact on outcomes that may be far-reaching for generations—on corporate or organizational design, government law or statute, judicial opinion, school policy, or public policy.

QL Leaders have established a personal legacy that grows over time as they continue to expand their influence. While few people ever leave a public legacy, Leaders who are founders of organizations or have held C-level positions often have enduring reputations. On the walls of corporate headquarters, you may find their framed photos, buildings may be named after them, or they may have authored influential articles, white papers, and books. Their historical record comprises overcoming countless obstacles and accumulating a long list of achievements. They've innovated, made groundbreaking discoveries, and left their positive mark on the industries where they've worked. Through their Leadership, they have inspired those within their organizations to carry on their vision. Before they enter a conference room or Zoom meeting, participants eagerly await these Leaders' insights and contributions and have confidence in their experience, knowledge, and judgment.

To successfully operate as a powerbroker, Leaders consider opposing positions. They study counterarguments and adapt a new position if they believe it's superior to theirs. Or they effectively argue against a position if, after thorough analysis, they believe it's inferior. In discussions with powerbrokers, a back-and-forth between point and counterpoint is common. Within this level of exchange, winning or losing is not relevant—that is the preoccupation of an ordinary leader who is not confident in his or her power and thereby views each debate with a need to win at any cost. Rather, with a QL Leader, both parties remain focused on the goal of sharing and promoting thoughts on the best course of action to take. Leaders are confident in their own power, have found peace in their wisdom and perspective, and therefore are above verbal battles that will take away from their serenity.

Powerbrokers' tools are their knowledge, resources, and experience. When they take the quantum leap, they do so as professionals already known for their achievements. While they do not have to prove themselves successful again, they eagerly take on new challenges with poise and self-assurance. As tough as the work is ahead of them, they take great pleasure in what they do to the degree that they characterize their professional paths as a downright fun adventure. They proceed fearlessly, feeling no need to prove themselves by adding another accomplishment to their résumé. With their reputations already established, they focus on setting and reaching ambitious goals, leveraging their unparalleled networks, and mobilizing others to join their cause. With a long line of loyal followers, powerbrokers are able to enlist highly motivated and successful individuals that will propel them forward as they make their quantum leap.

Only a relatively small number of Leaders successfully take the quantum leap. In fact, most people in leadership positions become better at what they do over the years and are quite content ending their professional careers and transitioning to a comfortable retirement without ever taking the quantum leap.

By no means should those who have enjoyed productive leadership careers be expected to go on forever and into new industries. The purpose of embarking on a discussion of QL Leaders in this book is not to suggest that every successful professional should hold this as a goal. People who have worked hard and had more successes than failures are well deserving of respect. After years of rising at dawn, working well into the night, studying mountains of data and reports, collaborating with every kind of person imaginable, and so often making deep personal sacrifices for the good of the cause, only a remarkable person would opt to continue working endlessly with the same amount of energy and passion in another industry.

In fact, Leaders who eschew becoming a QL Leader may do so for multiple reasons that benefit themselves, their industries, and those around them, including their family members. Taking the quantum leap for a new challenge without proper preparation and motives may result in a failed quantum leap that benefits no one. But when Leaders commit to taking this rare journey and succeed, their status as a QL Leader demonstrates the limitless potential of the human mind within a free, open, and prosperous society.

The Master Leader

A QL Leader excels in multiple sectors and has established a lasting legacy. Those Leaders that take the step beyond the QL Leader become Master Leaders. In the *Star Wars* series, Yoda is a Jedi master who served as the grand master of the Jedi Council.[2] He taught as a Jedi for eight hundred years, and through his connection to the Force, he had unlocked the path to greatness and immortality. A mentor of all mentors, he led by example, drew out the best in those who sought his wisdom, and inspired others to reach their highest potential. Within Leadership, reaching Yoda status is the pinnacle.

QL Leadership is the prerequisite to Master Leadership, and not all QL Leaders take the leap. The Master Leader's strengths comprise all that QL Leadership entails and includes further intellectual and spiritual development. The vision that Master Leaders develop runs so deep that it can result in prophetic wisdom.

Master Leaders do not pontificate, require those whose insight they seek to follow it, or tell others what to do. Rather, they steer others to gaining deeper empathy and higher levels of understanding of themselves. When those they coach apply a Master Leader's teaching, they benefit the organization and people around them.

Having spent their adult lives voraciously learning, Master Leaders reach a place of peace and serenity that is drastically different from the high energy, bold, and sometimes frenzied activity of the emerging Leader. They navigate through life with less volatility and more tranquility than in their prior Leadership stages.

The Master Leader works with those who seek the next stage of growth but can't identify what it is. These men and women aren't at the start of their Leadership journey. Rather, like the Jedi, they are far along their path and already Leaders. They've accomplished a great deal, but

2 "Yoda," Star Wars Databank, accessed November 19, 2024, https://www.starwars.com/databank/yoda.

they're not connecting with an intuitive sense of what is next. Even high-level Leaders with long track records can experience this dilemma. This is where Master Leaders help discern what lies ahead. They could provide guidance into how you handle the position you're in, change your present position, or perform a different kind of work entirely.

Although effective and successful Leaders have a strong ability to articulate a vision that will guide their followers, they may be less adept in identifying the next step in their own journeys. What vision do they hold for themselves? Having achieved a great deal, their thoughts may be best described by the famous song "Is That All There Is?" Determining next steps is a continual responsibility.

This doesn't imply that a Leader must move from one position or organization to another. Rather, it suggests that one's personal, most intimate, and private development has yet to be determined. One may remain within an organization for many years, continuing to grow and change. The work of the Master Leader is to support, encourage, and guide Leaders at all levels to find their path to self-realization.

The impact Master Leaders have on the many people they work with is profound, often inspiring people far beyond a Leader's lifetime.

Throughout history, many individuals with religious stripes have been easily identified as Master Leaders—among them Jesus, Mahatma Ghandi, Buddha, Mohammed, and Mother Teresa. It is easy to see how they influenced others. But by no means are all Master Leaders of a religious bent or as easily recognizable. Master Leaders possess a wisdom and calm that quietly persists in the support and development of others. They may be found in organizations, institutions, community groups, and even the extended family unit.

Summary

I have spent years visiting and observing organizations of all sizes representing many sectors, as well as thousands of hours speaking with both veteran leaders and aspiring ones. Repeatedly, I'm asked a version of the following:

How do I become a successful leader and climb the positional leadership ladder?

Within these pages, you've learned my vision of high-achievement leadership. For me, there are multiple ways to be a Leader, and positional Leadership is only one of them. Nevertheless, it's the leadership path I'm most often asked about, most likely because people identify success with a job title such as CFO, COO, or CEO.

Successful Leadership is highly subjective and goes beyond measuring accomplishment by one's position within an organization. In this book, I've provided guidelines that align with my perspective, experience, and insights about successful work within an organization.

I'm a strong believer in simplicity. Heading a high-achieving organization requires sophisticated professional skills, one of which is simplifying otherwise complicated concepts. In particular, part of bringing people on your side is expressing your vision and aspirations, as well as your challenges, in the most straightforward manner possible. Motivating others to follow your lead requires a masterful ability to make the complex easy to understand. Even the most sophisticated audience has limited patience in hearing and committing to a creative thought that requires action. Engaging people is not only required; it is also a constant. A Leader focused on improvement and growth must always rigorously seek better ways of turning outlined expectations into accomplished goals.

The foundation of Leadership is largely built on basic but often overlooked principles. Although the workplace has changed over time and this evolution has rapidly accelerated as a result of the coronavirus, fundamental leadership principles are both timeless and still relevant.

On the one hand, the widespread trend of working from home presents new challenges, and the consequences are still to be determined. On the other hand, such a dramatic change still requires Leaders to set expectations and uphold performance standards that transcend any current workplace movement.

Sadly, there is a trend of disregarding the perspective of seasoned Leaders. But as long as they are evolving, adapting, and producing positive outcomes, their insights and recommendations are timely and relevant.

The high-performing workplace is never stagnant. Leaders are charged to balance the old and the new. They are responsible to shape the workplace. With the board of directors, Leaders engage in research that improves and supports the organization's growth.

In the case of my organization, I work with my board of directors to improve school environments and support the development of leadership theory for all American institutions and organizations.

This book on Leadership reflects the culmination of decades gaining wisdom and experience from establishing a high-performing, award-winning organization. Writing this book moved me beyond acquiring insight to taking the bold step of presenting my perspective to the rest of the world. The guidance I've provided in these pages has improved the lives of countless individuals both inside and far beyond the campuses of our organization.

Leadership Storm provides advice for those in a broad range of sectors. The organizations they work for may be large, medium, or small. Given today's flexible economy, they may even be individual operators of online businesses. The culture of an organization may be highly formal or informal in terms of structure and day-to-day protocols. Regardless of your specific sector, the core concepts you've read about are essential for your success in managing people in any part of your organization.

Practice the information you've found valuable. Disregard what you've identified as not relevant to your situation, but carefully consider why and make sure this is actually the case. Upon further examination, you may realize that information you initially discounted is actually relevant and worthy of your attention. In either case, keep *Leadership Storm* handy so you can access a specific chapter or section when you find yourself having to address a problem identified in this book.

There is a popular saying: "Amateurs work until they get it right. Professionals work until they can't get it wrong." Whether you're just beginning in your career or have gained the status of Yoda, there's no finish line to cross because the journey of growth has no end.

Working and collaborating with people carries a responsibility that requires a high level of commitment, endless energy, an ethical framework, and a sincere and authentic willingness to engage in a compassionate way.

The process of self-actualization goes hand in hand with operating as a successful Leader. In my case, I cherish the insights, ideas, and advice I have received from extraordinary Leaders from the military, businesses of all kinds, the healthcare industry, government, elected office, and education, my own field. In the future, I believe truly excellent Leaders will not be bound to one sector. Instead, their expertise and capabilities will allow them to move fluidly between various fields.

No matter how leadership theory continues to evolve, without a doubt, it is the most bold, righteous, and visionary Leaders that play a major role in shaping a healthy, compassionate, and prosperous future for all organizations and the people within them.

Best and heartfelt wishes for extraordinary success throughout your Leadership journey.

ACKNOWLEDGMENTS

THERE ARE DOZENS of individuals that have contributed to this effort. Here I recognize some of the key people who made this book possible.

Lawrence Ineno was my editor. He supported the writing of this second effort at inspiring and guiding others to growth and change. Although his professional background differs from mine, we share a common point of view. Lawrence was an inspiration. He allowed me to explore, helped to insert self-discipline into the process, and challenged the thinking at every turn. A previous bestselling author on his own, he understood the expectation and kept the work focused until we fulfilled the vision for it.

Thanks to the following individuals who have shared their leadership stories and journeys with this author. Their mentorship of others has positively affected more lives than can be readily understood or quantified.

RADM Leendert Hering, USN, Retired, Scott Barton, Eric Schweinfurter, Dr. David Crean, Tim Morton, Wayland Meyers, Jim Herr, Steve McNulty, Lynne Alipio, Tim Tuter, Tiffany Yandell, Wade Aschbrenner,

Denise Shields, Dr. Vickie Barber, Dr. Arlene Gluck, and Dr. Tom Davis have all demonstrated excellent models for fostering leadership in others and have served as a great support to me in my work.

This book was originally developed as a training manual. The schools I founded not only focus on the delivery of high-quality instruction to students seeking an individualized and personalized path to learning but also support research and leadership training for all staff. For over thirty years, the board of directors at Altus Schools have been extremely supportive of efforts to create innovative approaches to teaching and learning. In recent years, they called for formal documentation of what our organization has learned.

The initial assignment was to expand our strategic planning to include investigation into where the future was taking public education. Later, as I presented the results and came to understand that other people wanted to know more, the board asked me to document my philosophy, perspectives, and personal insights in the form of a trilogy of books and trainings. This is the second in a series leading to critical points for consideration.

Even amid an extraordinary period of rapid change, there remain some basics that form a foundation for people seeking a highly successful, productive, and public leadership role in their life's work. The wisdom shared in *Leadership Storm* is meant to inform the individual journeys embarked upon by all its readers.

Author photograph by Altus Schools

ABOUT THE AUTHOR

MARY SEARCY BIXBY, MED, founder and superintendent of nine California charter schools, is widely recognized at the state, national, and international levels for her cutting-edge and bold educational reform leadership. She created the Altus Model for Organizational Leadership that focuses on improvement and high performance. A sought-after keynote speaker and advisor, Mary provides expertise in leadership training, educational reform, and the management of processes oriented toward organizational peak performance.

A former school principal and administrator, Mary fulfilled her mission of providing quality educational options to neighborhoods across Southern California by founding the Altus Schools in 1994. In 2015, the United States secretary of commerce presented one of eight schools Mary founded, The Charter School of San Diego (CSSD), with the Malcolm Baldrige National Quality Award. It is the only performance excellence award given by the United States Office of the President. CSSD was the first K through 12 school in America to receive this honor. In 2021, the school received its second Baldrige National Award, an honor only a handful of organizations have ever achieved.

Mary has been repeatedly recognized for her futuristic vision and high-achieving leadership. Among her numerous recognitions and honors are the following: In 2024, she received the E. David Spong Lifetime Achievement Award. This award is presented in recognition of an individual who has performed truly extraordinary service and has created a positive and lasting legacy. She received the Harry S. Hertz Award, which recognizes a person whose behavior inspires, encourages, challenges, and empowers others to achieve performance excellence. Her breakthrough contributions to education have earned her the Remarkable Leaders in Education award from the University of San Diego School of Leadership and Education. Vistage, a twenty-one-thousand-member business-advisory and executive-coaching organization that spans twenty countries, also recognized her sterling leadership.

The California Charter Schools Association honored Mary with both the Hart Vision Award and its Legacy Award. She was a recipient of the Inspirational School Leader Award from the Charter School Development Center. Mary has twice been a finalist for *San Diego Business Journal*'s Women Who Mean Business for her contributions to education and the community.

On a personal level, Mary has received the Charles Francis Buddy Award, presented to an individual who embodies the mission and values of the University of San Diego; exhibits extraordinary contributions and commitment to humanitarian causes; promotes human welfare, rights, and dignity; and advocates peace, justice, and freedom.

Her current projects include the introduction of a California Teacher Induction program into Altus University, a university program for educational professionals within a K through 12 charter school. She is leading a team creating opportunities for humanoid robot instruction as a tool to be used by teachers for small group instruction within Altus Schools.

Mary, whose professional writing and research center on Altus culture and achievement, is the author of *Charter Storm: Waves of Change Sweeping over Public Education,* which captures her experience and views relating to charter schools. She is currently working on her third book, which focuses on the creation and implementation of the Altus Model for Organizational Leadership.

Mary and her husband enjoy family gatherings, sports and theater events, gardening, and music.